The RV Lifestyle

# Conquer The Road

## RV Maintenance for Travelers

**Margo Armstrong**

## Conquer the Road – RV Maintenance for Travelers

The author and publisher have made their best effort to produce a high quality, informative and helpful book. They make no representation or warranties of any kind with regard to the completeness or accuracy of the contents of the book. They accept no liability of any kind for losses or damages caused or alleged to be caused, directly or indirectly, from using the information contained in this book.

ISBN: 978-0692246740

# From the Author

You have heard many times, "take care of your vehicle and it takes care of you." That type of care and maintenance is the focus of this book. *"Conquer the Road - RV Maintenance for Travelers"* provides assistance to help **you** maintain your RV.

Also included: RV driving tips, weight balance information for cargo, and seasonal storage input.

For me, an overview of how things work makes all the difference. *Conquer the Road: RV Maintenance for Travelers* steps through the basic RV maintenance procedures with plenty of photos.

Enjoy!

*Margo Armstrong*

# Contents

**From the Author**............................................................ iii

**Introduction**................................................................... 1

   Electricity and Safety ................................................. 3

   Test Equipment to Have On Hand .......................... 4

**Self-Maintenance** ........................................................ 5

**Pre- Purchase Checkout** ........................................... 7

**Maintaining the "Look"** ............................................11

**Dealing with the Repair Shop** ............................... 13

**Windshield Wipers**.................................................... 15

**Awning**........................................................................ 17

   Maintenance Guide................................................. 18

**Roof Maintenance** ..................................................... 21

   Repairing the Roof.................................................. 22

   Types of Roof Repair .............................................. 23

   Replacing the Roof Coating................................... 25

   How To Find The Source Of A Leak .................... 26

   Moisture Meter........................................................ 27

**Air Conditioner** ......................................................... 29

   Maintenance Procedures......................................... 30

**Managing Power, AC and DC**.................................. 31

   Line Monitor............................................................ 31

   Power Manager ....................................................... 32

   Electrical System Protection ................................... 34

Circuit Breakers and Fuse Boxes.......................... 34

Approximately AMP Ratings.............................. 36

Electric Cable Adapter for External Use ............. 38

*50- to 30-amp Adapter....................................................39*

*30- to 50-amp Adapter....................................................40*

## Batteries ................................................................... 41

Engine Battery ................................................. 41

Coach Batteries................................................. 41

Find the Right Size Battery for Your Rig ............. 43

Battery Maintenance............................................. 45

Solar Panel for Battery Charging ........................ 46

## The Basics of Solar Technology........................... 47

Rating Solar Panels ............................................. 49

Quality of Solar Panels...................................... 50

Basic Requirements for Panels ........................... 50

Controllers ....................................................... 50

Basic Regulating Technologies............................ 51

*Shunt and Pulse Width Modulation ...........................51*

*Temperature Compensation..................................52*

## Inverter ................................................................... 53

## Converter................................................................. 55

## Generator ............................................................... 59

Maintenance Procedures................................... 61

## Sewer System ........................................................ 63

Sewer Hose ....................................................... 63

Tips For A Happy Toilet...................................... 65

*Emptying the Gray and Black Water Tanks.................65*

*Routine Tank-dumping Procedure* ................................ *67*

*Black Water Tank Maintenance* ..................................... *69*

*Gray Water Tank Maintenance* ...................................... *71*

## Propane Tank ................................................. **73**

## Hot Water Heater ............................................ **75**
Use Electric Only or Combination ........................ 75
Troubleshooting the Water Heater ....................... 76

## Water Pump ................................................... **83**
Pump Not Working ................................................. 85

## Fresh Water Tank ........................................... **87**
Sanitizing the Fresh Water System ....................... 88

## Refrigerator ................................................. **91**
Things You Can Do to Keep It Cool .................... 94
Routine Refrigerator Maintenance ....................... 98
Refrigerator Not Working .................................... 100
Boondocking Tips ................................................. 102

## Furnace ....................................................... **103**
Furnace Not Working or Operating Correctly . 105

## Filtering Your Water ...................................... **107**
Exterior Water Filter ............................................ 107
Drinking Water Filters ......................................... 108
Drinking Water Hoses and Connectors ............. 109

## Towing Your Car ........................................... **113**

## Motorhome Tires ........................................... **117**
Rotation and Alignment .................................... 120

## Hydraulic Leveling Systems ........................... **121**
Maintenance Procedures ..................................... 123

**Chassis**................................................................. **123**
Wheel Bearings........................................ 125
Axels, Brakes, Differential ........................ 125
Engine Transmission ................................ 126
Engine Belts and Hoses............................ 126
RV Slideouts ............................................ 126

**Hot Weather Tips** .................................... **129**
Refrigerator.............................................. 129
Interior Wood Cabinets............................. 131
Window Shields ........................................ 131

**Storing Your RV** ........................................ **133**

**Driving Tips** .............................................. **137**
Proper Braking Technique........................ 137
Understanding the Gears.......................... 138
Speed Limits ............................................ 139
Adjusting Outside Mirrors ........................ 140
Cargo Weight Balance ............................. 142
Liquid Weights (Pounds Per Gallon)......... 145

**Other eBooks by Margo Armstrong** .............. **146**

———————————◆———————————

# Introduction

A part of living the RV lifestyle is learning how to maintain your recreational vehicle and it is also part of the fun.

Staying on top of the important maintenance issues includes understanding how the separate systems work.

Keeping good records and setting up a calendar for future maintenance keeps your RV on the road and the driver calm and happy.

Following a few simple procedures in a timely manner can keep your older RV "looking new." With these same procedures, your new RV keeps that "look" for many years.

**Before the first trip:**

☑ Take the RV in for a complete service. This service is usually the most expensive of all future maintenance, as you want everything checked including the axles and brakes. (Ignore this suggestion if you had a thorough *pre-purchase checkout* done earlier.)

▶ Even if right off the dealer's lot, this new RV probably drove several thousand miles to get to its new home.

▶ Even if brand new, quality control may have missed something vital when testing at the end of the manufacturing line. This is a good time to find out if you have a "lemon."

▶ Vibration from rolling down the highway to the sales lot, hitting potholes and debris, and swaying in the wind are all factors that can lead to problems.

▶ Keep in mind that **if** the RV sits in storage for six to eight months out of the year, extra vigilance is needed (more on this later).

☑ Complete the *Motorhome Component Information* form. All the information about your rig is in one place, right at your fingertips when researching, ordering, or buying parts.

Unfortunately, this book is not the platform to distribute 8 x 11 forms. To download the free PDF template for *"My Motorhome Component Information,"* please visit my webpage:

**http://RVMaintenance.MovingOnWithMargo.com.**

# Electricity and Safety

A few words about working with electricity:

- Never substitute electrical components without professional inspection. If changing fuse size, replacing breakers, or wire size, make sure a professional electrician checks out the final project.
- Never bypass a circuit protection device.
- Before attempting any repairs, make sure the power is disconnected.
- Never work on an electrical system before you know what and where the power source is located.
- Never probe with a test light or a multimeter without knowing the kind of voltage.
- Excessive heat is the number one killer of power. Brown-outs (very low power) contribute the most to equipment damage as they force the equipment to work beyond their safety margin.

# Maintenance Schedule

Incorporating regular care and maintenance into your schedule can produce many carefree years with your RV.

Some of the topics covered in *Conquer the Road – RV Maintenance for Travelers*:

- Pre-Purchase Checkout
- Maintaining the "Look"
- Dealing with the Repair Shop
- Air Conditioner, Refrigerator, Hot Water Heater

- Batteries, Inverter, Basic Solar Technology
- Sewer System
- Water Pump, Filtering Your Water
- Furnace
- Hydraulic Leveling System
- Awning
- Roof Maintenance
- Electrical System Protection

## Test Equipment to Have On Hand

- Plug-in Meter to read voltage and polarity (See *Managing Power* for a recommendation).
- Test light, or digital meter, for 12 volt systems.
- Multimeter, analog or digital, for testing continuity and resistance.

---◆---

# Self-Maintenance

The best maintenance is that performed by you. Not only is it cost effective, it gives you a sense of control over this huge machine and its components.

The first step is setting up a maintenance calendar. Do this on your computer with a follow-up reminder, or manually on a wall calendar. If you have *Microsoft*™ *Outlook*®, its *Task* feature works perfectly as a reminder.

Keep in mind that taking care of your RV pays off in comfort for you and possibly a big resale value when it is time to move on. Start the cycle by buying quality and maintaining it properly. A quality-built recreational vehicle can retain its showroom glow twenty years later if properly cared for in a timely manner.

- Learn how to perform the basic maintenance yourself by taking courses offered by various RV support groups.
- Escapees RV Club has quarterly events that offer maintenance seminars. **http://www.escapees.com**

▶ Create checklists for engine, transmission, and battery maintenance.

▶ Purchase the necessary tools to change the oil and filters. If outsourcing this, know the correct oil/filter specifications so the service personnel are not likely to make mistakes.

▶ Read the manufacturer's manuals provided with your rig, and secure necessary manuals from other sources when necessary.

You may have to contact several vendors to accumulate all the information you need for maintenance. Use the Internet to download manuals.

▶ Carry spare parts for on-the-spot repairs.

▶ Depending on the size of your rig, carry a spare tire and wheel.

▶ If you have a wood interior, be prepared to keep conditioning agents on-board. There are several gel-type applications that keep the mess and smell to a minimum. Linseed oil is one type to avoid.

▶ Read the manufacturer's guide and create a checklist to keep the refrigerator, stove, and air conditioning units in top shape. If you buy used, be prepared to contact the manufacturer for these guides, most are available free online.

# Pre- Purchase Checkout

Before you purchase any RV, **always, always, always** have an independent RV mechanic checkout the vehicle before you sign on the dotted line. This process can save you a lot of headaches and money later.

Minimum pre-purchase examination checklist:

- Air Conditioners (roof and engine-driven)
- Awning
- Batteries (test for life cycle)
- Engine
- Hydraulic levelers
- Propane system (test for leaks)
- Roof coating and seals around vents, air conditioner, antennas
- Slideout seals (if applicable)
- Refrigerator
- Water Heater
- Window seals

- Coach Door locks
- Retractable step
- Tire life & manufactured date

Things you can check yourself:

- Microwave
- Window shades or blinds
- Water flow
- Toilet
- Light fixtures

Some RV repair shops offer a free checkout service, hoping they can charge the owner to fix the items that wind up on their checklist. Other shops might charge $100 to spend the hour necessary. You may be able to negotiate with the owner to pay for the fixes, or drop the price.

If you purchase through an RV dealer, this independent pre-purchase checkout may become an issue, so be prepared. Always arrange to be onsite personally during the inspection to ensure that the checklist is completed.

Do not skip this step no matter what tale the sales person spins. If they refuse to cooperate, walk away. Know there is something terribly wrong with the RV, regardless of the exterior/interior appearance.

The point being that usually people trade in their RVs when they begin to suspect that they need to spend thousands of dollars on repairs. Dealers take these vehicles in trade usually without regard to condition.

The dealer's profit margin is so high on the newer RV they just sold this customer, they can afford to do this. If the exterior is presentable, they sell the trade to some unsuspecting newbie. Beware!

This is similar to the way people value their automobiles. If they really enjoy a vehicle, they continue to keep up the maintenance until it overwhelms them with repair costs. If it is junk to start with, they get rid of it sooner rather than later. This makes complete sense.

On the other hand, some people sell their RV simply because they want a new feature, a new layout, a diesel rather than a gas engine. Some sell because of ill health. These are the preferred RVs to purchase. If possible, buy your first RV from this type of owner.

# Notes:

# Maintaining the "Look"

Once you find the perfect RV, enjoy keeping the exterior paint fresh and glossy. It is pleasing to the eye and ups the resale value enormously.

Preventing roof runoff, those black streaks, from fouling up the sidewall paint may not be possible, but you can keep these streaks from embedding into the exterior paint by waxing often. The new spray "auto detail" waxes available now do an excellent job and are easy to apply. Spray on, wipe off.

If the body sidewalls are fiberglass, not aluminum, upkeep is more difficult. Generally, it requires a liquid wax, such as *Nu Finish*, to add some shine.

While you are sitting outside enjoying the view, keep an eye on the exterior condition of the RV. Not allowing dirt and bird dropping stains to accumulate on the paint job keeps your RV looking almost showroom perfect.

Depending on the size of your RV, a complete wash and wax job can be exhausting. However, spending an hour a week touching up with a spray wax makes all the difference in the "look."

Installing the proper side gutters on your RV, to direct the runoff from the air conditioner and rainfall, could prove worth the money, since gutters save time keeping the "look" alive.

# Dealing with the Repair Shop

With all the horror stories floating around about the RV repair business, who can you trust to take care of major repairs or install add-ons to personalize your RV?

- Ask at the RV park front desk for reliable services that guests have recommended.
- Always ask for a written work order with the repairs or services written down and a cost estimate explained in detail.
- Have them place *right on the work order* that any extra costs over $100 require a phone call and approval from you **before** any work is performed.
- *Ensure that you walk away with a copy of the completed work order.*
- Do not hesitate to discuss the final bill with the shop owner if you have a problem with it.
- If the shop refuses to follow your guidelines, find another vendor.

▶ The most expensive and frustrating project of them all is woodworking and cabinet making. Finding a quality artisan that can fulfill your dream is difficult.

Keep looking until you get a referral from someone that actually has personal experience with the artisan. Stay an extra week or month, if necessary.

If possible, take a look at a finished project to see if it meets your expectation. After finding the right artist, expect to spend several weeks awaiting the end result.

(Avoid this experience altogether by spending the money upfront when purchasing your first RV and buy quality.)

▶ A word to the wise: Before making any expensive cosmetic changes, make sure you are happy enough with your first RV to keep it for a few years.

Any upgrades you make now are most likely not going to render any monetary gain when you sell it. Try to hold down the tendency to re-decorate until you live in it for at least six months.

---

# Windshield Wipers

*Ron McNevin shared this great tip in Motorhome Magazine.*

"Windshield wiper blades can be quite expensive to replace. I discovered a cheap way to provide UV protection.

I bought 3/8- to 1/2-inch foam pipe insulation, cut it in half and wrapped it around the blades. Now I have protection for the wipers and it cost me less than $2."

Great idea, Ron, one I share myself. When on the road, in dry weather, you can even drive with them installed.

Finding the correct replacement wiper size can be a time consuming project. If possible, put wiper replacement on the list when the next service cycle comes up. Let the mechanic do the research and replacement.

Sometimes it takes a trip to a large RV sales and service establishment to find the correct windshield wiper replacement. Once you find it, write down the part number and manufacturer on the *Motorhome Component List,* ready for easy replacement next time.

# Awning

Taking care of the patio and window awnings is one of those essential tasks. There are two types of material used in your average awning material construction, acrylic and vinyl.

Each type has its own specifications for maintenance. Vinyl is the easiest to care for, as soap and water works fine.

Vinyl, however, does not endure as long as acrylic, nor does it have the colorful, rich look of the fabric.

Since acrylic is not waterproof, caring for this awning fabric requires a specially formulated cleaning agent. Try *Woolite*® as it contains no bleach, phosphates, or harsh enzymes.

This special care detergent prevents opening the weave of the fabric and allowing moisture to accumulate. There are other specialty cleaners available too.

Keep in mind that mildew does not form on the awning material itself, but on the dust and debris allowed to accumulate on the fabric. Keeping the awning clean eliminates that issue.

## Maintenance Guide

1. When opening the awning for the first time, note the condition of the awning arms, roller, and the fabric.

2. Each time you open the awning, take note of the condition. Catching little signs of damage can prevent having to replace the fabric.

3. To keep the fabric from stretching during the rainy season, lower one arm of the awning, allowing the rain to drain off rather than pool in the middle.

   If the awning starts to sag with the water overload, it causes the roller to bend. Rolling up the awning then becomes a problem that can only be solved by replacing parts or the complete awning itself.

4. Keep an eye on the weather. During predicted high winds, always roll the awning up. Updrafts can literally tear the awning off the vehicle.

5. When traveling, always secure the arms with Velcro straps to keep the material from unfurling in high winds.

6. Paying extra money to ensure that your awning has an aluminum or vinyl shield is wise.

 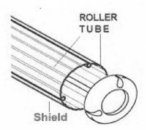

ROLLER
TUBE

Shield

7. Without a shield attached, it is always a good idea to use a tie down strap for the middle of the awning when traveling.

8. When at the campsite, use a set of "de-flappers" to attach the loose part of the awning to the arm. This stretches the center part of the fabric and prevents it from flapping in the wind.

9. Apply Silicone lubricant to the threaded shafts of all black locking knobs to resist corrosion.

10. Use a spray silicone lubricant on all sliding parts and knobs.

11. Check all arm pivot points for enlargement of holes or broken rivets.

12. Check the awning fabric for loose stitching and possible shrinkage or puckering. A local awning repair shop may be needed.

13. When closing the awning ensure that the awning pull down strap is evenly distributed along the roller.

# Roof Maintenance

At least twice a year, clean the RV roof with detergent and water. Sometimes the entire roof is black from dirt, debris, and composted leaves. Scrub using a stiff brush and rinse thoroughly with water.

If you have aluminum or fiberglass siding on your RV, the popping sound you hear from time to time is the chassis structure flexing. This is caused from temperature change and simply traveling down the road. This flexing requires that the roof covering be flexible too. Aging and lack of maintenance can create a costly roof replacement at some point.

Keep a close watch on the condition of the roof. Even rubber and PermaSeal roofs need attention. Leaks are the greatest cause of wood rot and structure failure, not to mention ugly discoloration of the interior headliner.

- Check for cracks caused by sunlight exposure and the normal flexing of the chassis.
- Check around all the vents, skylights and air conditioner for cracks.

> The biggest hazard is where the fiberglass caps attach to the front and rear of the roof. When those seals crack, usually at the corners, from vibration, heat, and cold stress, water leaks down into the interior walls.

# Repairing the Roof

Mentioned here are a few products that are used currently to permanently seal the roof and have a minimum of 5- to 10–year warranties. Before using any of these products, remove all previous sealants, tapes, caulking and patches. Wash and scrub the roof with a firm bristle brush to remove all residue. Some products require a primer.

*Suggestion*: If you are doing the repair job yourself, for small leaks that are not in the cap seams, start with the EternaBond Doublestick tape.

> First, find where the water is leaking into the interior (see *How To Find The Source of a Link*).

> Spend the time to clean the area thoroughly first with a stiff brush and rinse, or the tape does not seal.

If you purchase a used RV and the roof is leaking, consider spending the money to have a professional roof coating applied before wood rot creates a completely new problem. This ensures the end of leaks. Unfortunately just patching with a Dicor sealant or EternaBond tape is a short-term approach for a long-term problem.

# Types of Roof Repair

**PermaSeal**: an elastic polyurethane coating that resembles rubber. It is sprayed seamlessly over any roof surface. Spraying right up to the edge of vents, skylights and over the cap seams on each end of the roof, it eliminates any possibility of leaks. As it is impervious to humidity, mold and fungus, this coating has a long life. With reasonable care taken not to slice or cut this thick covering, leaks are a thing of the past.

When sprayed on it dries within 15 minutes. PermaSeal is available in 24-oz. aerosol cans, gallons or professionally sprayed over the entire roof. This coating can be painted when dry. Lasts 10 years or more before recoating required.

**RoofMate:** an elastomeric Acrylic roof coating with high tensile strength. Non-flammable, easy roll-on application, and quick curing, it is suitable for about 6 years before applying a recoat. Prime before using.

**Ultra Shield**: An elastomeric acrylic roof coating. Easy to apply (roll-on), quick cure, and non-flammable, it comes in several standard colors. Suitable for about 5 years before recoat. Prime before using.

**EternaBond Doublestick** tape: Used extensively for small roof repairs. Unfortunately, this tape does not work well on the cap seams and cannot be used over silicone products.

**Dicor Ultra Sealant:** A high performance adhesive/sealant. Providing excellent, long lasting superior adhesion and durability, Dicor is similar in appearance to caulking. It is applied the same way with a caulking gun. This sealant can be used for TPO roofing.

Often mobile repair businesses use this sealant to stop leaks, as it is inexpensive and quick to apply. It must be applied smoothly and not in goopy chunks (shown below) that crack with temperature changes, breaking the seal. It must be pressed down so it flows into and seals the cracks.

Not a good application of sealant.

## Replacing the Roof Coating

The only problem found when doing the pre-purchase check on my current used motorhome was the roof and some fiberglass damage in the rear. The owner promised to fix the roof and discounted the purchase price for the exterior damage. Experience tells us to follow up on any repairs.

As it turned out, he used EternaBond on the cap seams that, of course, did not hold. I spent several hundred dollars on Dicor sealant repair jobs, but nothing worked. Finally, I spent the money to get a *PermaSeal* roof (longest warranty). Problem now solved, for at least 10 years.

After spraying on the basic black coating, they run the coating (by hand brush) right up to the vents and skylight edges, sealing off any possible leaks. Then the white reflective paint is rolled on.

They used EternaBond to reinforce the skylight seams.

# How To Find The Source Of A Leak

According to Curtis Carter at *FunTimesGuide.com*:

"The first step should be a good water test — one that takes some time, as you may need to allow the water to travel its path before you see it coming into the interior space. I recommend using a garden hose with the nozzle set on a wide spray."

This definitely is a two-person project. Be patient with the process. One person apparently stands on the inside watching and the other sprays water along all the seams, roof vents, and even the siding itself.

Be sure to run water around the air conditioner gasket as it can migrate to other spots under the roof.

If you start the water test from the ground up, you know where the leak originates. If the leak is in a vertical seam or later coming from the roof, it becomes obvious.

## Moisture Meter

One tool I find to be very helpful is a reliable moisture meter. This is one way to find out if water is pooling somewhere out of sight. If you find wood rot, fix it before recoating the roof.

The General MMD4E Moisture Meter works well for wood and concrete.

# Water Pressure Leaks

If the leaks appear to be coming from under the RV, it may just be a temporary leak from too much pressure on the water lines.

It is impossible to judge the water pressure coming from the RV parks faucet without some type of pressure gauge.

There are several types of water pressure regulators on the market. My recommendation is the more expensive stainless steel version because it does not rust.

All of the types shown above are pre-set to 45 psi flowing to the RV, even if there is a visual gauge attached. There is one model that I found that does allow you to adjust the pressure (very expensive).

While you are shopping, pick up a few filter washers for the regulator. These washers often are destroyed by contaminants in the water. When setting up, remember to let the water flow for a few seconds to rinse any pent up debris before attaching the regulator.

# Air Conditioner

A roof mounted RV air conditioner operates only on 120 V power. It requires at least a generator capable of providing 4000 watts to handle the startup energy necessary.

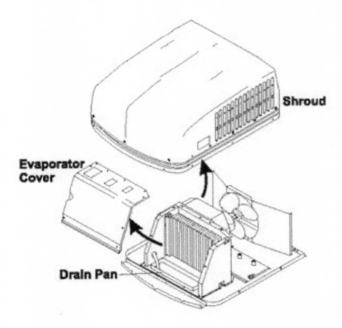

## Maintenance Procedures

▷ The inside filter should be checked and cleaned frequently. Use a gentle detergent, if any.

▷ Visually check the Roof gasket at least once a year. The gasket should be no less than $\frac{1}{2}$ -inch thick.

▷ Check and tighten Roof bolts, if necessary, at least once a year.

▷ Check the drain holes at least once a year.

▷ Check the evaporator coils for dirt and debris at least once a year.

▷ Inspect the rear fins on the back of the unit to ensure that they are not crushed.

# Managing Power, AC and DC

Vital components inside any RV manufactured after 1980, specifically those run by electronics, are exposed to sudden termination by a low-power situation.

RV parks of all types, whether commercial or private resort, have problems at some point delivering 120 volts to your rig. Known as "brownouts," this condition is destructive.

## Line Monitor

▶ Purchase a *line monitor* with a digital readout that plugs into an AC outlet. Keep your eye on this meter to gauge the voltage available for use. Pay particular attention to this reading before turning on the microwave or air conditioning.

▶ Perform regular maintenance on the coach battery bank by keeping the distilled water at the proper level. Keep the electrolyte level stable as per the manufacturer's recommendations. (See *Batteries*.)

## Power Manager

Solve the low-power problem you find in older RV parks by purchasing a power manager. *PowerMaster* (recommended) or *Hughes Autoformer* are the most popular brands and available at some RV park stores.

These are very expensive ($350-$650) but are worth the investment if you live full-time or spend a season in your RV. Designed to handle most electrical problems, like surges, spikes and brownouts, these units also change the volt to amp ratio.

This heavy weather-resistant metal box primarily protects your RV equipment from damage caused by low power. This crisis is more commonly known as a "brownout."

Not just a power transformer, these units are designed to take any voltage spike and protect your RV's power systems.

A powerful enough spike burns out this unit instead of the microwave, air conditioner, or other appliance. Each manufacturer has a return plan in place should that burnout event occur.

From the *Power Master* and the *Autoformer* manufacturer's website:

*"The unit does not take power from the park. It does not affect the park or input voltage, or make electricity.*

*What it is doing is changing the voltage/amperage relationship, lowering the amperage and raising the voltage. Since appliances run better on higher voltage, lower amperage, less overall power is used from the park, and better service is enjoyed from your RV.*

*A unit running at full output (50 amps) uses 1 amp, but causes appliances to cycle more often and run cooler. This uses less total power from the park.*

▶ 30 and 50 Amp models are available.

▶ As demand changes, the output adjusts.

▶ Run air conditioning and more of your appliances at the same time."

Get more information (and dealer locations) from the manufacturer:

▶ http://www.**PowerMasterRV.com**

▶ http://www.**AutoformersDirect.com**

## Electrical System Protection

If you choose not to use a *PowerMaster* or *Autoformer*, some type of protection needs to be installed to protect your valuable appliances, TV, stereo and computers.

There are many options available. Find the one that fits your budget and gives the highest *joule* protection for spikes. It should also shut off the electric current if it drops below 104 or above 132.

Pricing starts around $100 and accelerates to $350 for portable units providing full range protection. No voltage boosting is available with these units.

## Circuit Breakers and Fuse Boxes

One of the first things on your RV checklist is to find and label the circuit breakers and fuse boxes. They may be in separate locations or right next to each other.

Match each breaker to the location of the interior electric outlets so you know which breaker to move to the OFF position in a stress-related situation.

Remember, always disconnect the power before changing fuses. It is wise to carry extra fuses, but hire an electrician to replace a circuit breaker.

Find the GFCI (Ground Fault Circuit Interrupter) circuits inside and possibly one in the outside power cabinet, and label them. This is the first thing to check when the power to only one of the circuits in your RV shuts off. This may affect only one or two electrical outlets.

The kitchen and bathroom may have a GFCI. In addition, check the outlet connected to the inverter in the outside cabinet, if applicable.

Once you have located and corrected the reason for the shutoff, push the **Reset** button in and **hold for a few seconds** to re-start the power to this circuit.

# Approximate AMP Ratings

## 120 VAC

| Appliance | Amps |
|---|---|
| Air conditioner | 13 |
| Coffee maker | 12 |
| Water heater (electric) | 12 |
| Washer/dryer | 13 |
| Microwave | 8 |
| Convection | 15 |
| Refrigerator | 3.5 |
| Converter (charging) | 8 |
| Space heater (1600 watts) | 13 |
| Space heater (800 watts) | 6.5 |
| Iron | 8 |
| Electric blanket | 2 |
| Hair dryer (1500 watts) | 13 |
| Hair dryer (400 watts) | 3.5 |
| Curling iron | 0.7 |
| TV | .5-1.0 |
| VCR | 0.2 |
| Computer | 2 |

## 12 VDC

**Appliance or Accessory** .......................... **Estimated AMPs**

Aisle Light ................................................................1

CO Detector ..............................................................1

Fluorescent Light ................................................. 1-2

Furnace ............................................................. 10-12

LP Gas Leak Detector ........................................... 1

Overhead lights (Per Bulb)........................................1

Porch Light ............................................................. 1

Power Roof Vent ................................................... 1.5

Radio/Stereo ........................................................ 4

Range Hood (Fan & Light).................................... 2-3

Refrigerator (LP Gas Mode)................................ 1.5- 2

Security System .................................................... 1

Television (12 volt) ............................................. 4-5

TV Antenna Booster ............................................. <1

TV Antenna Booster 12 Volt outlet .....................Up to 8

Variable Speed Ceiling / Vent Fan...........................4

VCR Recorder / Player ...........................................2

Water Pump .............................................................4

## Electric Cable Adapter for External Use

RVs are designed either to run on a 30-amp or a 50-amp electrical connection. In one of the storage compartments outside is the *electrical bay*.

Inside is a long, thick cable wired into the RV that provides power to all the A/C electrical connections on the inside. This cable is plugged into the A/C power pedestal provided by the RV park or resort as part of their services.

Note that a 50-amp cable is very thick and heavy. Its plug has three prongs and a rounded ground prong.

A 30-amp cable is much thinner and lighter with two prongs and a rounded ground prong. (*See photo below.*)

For a more technical explanation, visit this link: **http://rvbasics.com/techtips/50-to-30-amp-adapter.html**

This A/C connection provides current to the air conditioner, microwave, all electrical outlets, and even some overhead interior lights.

All but some very old RV parks provide 30-amp service on a power pedestal somewhere on the site. 50-amp service is a relatively new upgrade for most parks and an extra service charge usually applies.

Some of the newer parks offer only 50-amp service. Others offer 30-amp and 50-amp service from the same post.

If your RV comes equipped with 50-amp service, then a 50- to 30-amp adapter should be a part of your electrical accessories. Most overnight stays between destinations are probably going to be in older parks.

Purchase an adapter that has a small length of cable between each end for ease of use. Plug the female end to your RV electrical cable, the male end to the power pedestal in the park.

**50- to 30-amp Adapter**

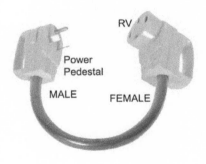

## 30- to 50-amp Adapter

If your RV uses a 30-amp cable, use a 30-to-50 amp adapter to be able to hook up to a 50-amp power pedestal. Simply plug in the female end of the adapter to your RV electrical cable and the male end to the 50-amp power pedestal on your site.

This **does not** give provide 50-amp service, but it does improve the quality of the voltage used.

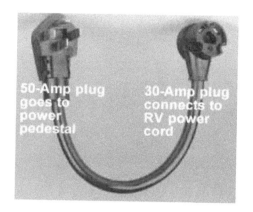

# Batteries

Many of the systems in an RV interact and one system can affect the performance of another. There are two different types of battery systems in any Class A or Class C motorhome.

## Engine Battery

Used primarily to start the engine, some motorhome manufacturers use this battery to power the radio and cockpit cigarette lighter sockets. Other manufacturers use the coach battery system for these same features.

It is wise to check the coach documentation and find out how your coach distributes this power system. It is important to keep this battery charged properly.

The engine battery is usually located near the generator or tucked in underneath the front hood like a car battery. It can be a sealed battery as it gets little use.

## Coach Batteries

Coach batteries are a different system that provides DC electricity to the interior of the coach, for example, the overhead vent fans and most of the interior lighting. If disconnected from any outside electrical source, these batteries provide all the current to the coach (see **Inverter**).

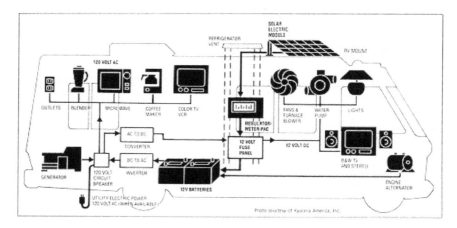

Coach batteries are usually located under the entrance steps or nearby outside compartment. These batteries are constantly being discharged by any interior demand requiring DC voltage.

There is still an ongoing debate about the best type of RV coach battery to purchase: Flooded acid (wet cells), gelled acid (gel cells) or AGM (absorbed glass mat).

The latest upgrade in coach batteries being tested for RV use is Lithium-Ion. Visit **http://www.technomadia.com/lithium** for all the details. It is an exciting dream to be able to carry all the power you need, indefinitely.

The quick answer is deep-cycle 12V flooded acid batteries. *Interstate* is the brand most commonly available (Sears, Wal-Mart) and reasonably priced.

Storage space dictates the actual number of batteries stored. If parking off the electrical grid beckons (boondocking), find more storage space nearby.

Almost all batteries supplied with new motorhomes are flooded acid batteries. If you purchase a large, high-end motorhome, it may have one of the other battery types.

Flooded acid batteries are the most common lead acid battery because they are cheaper and lighter in weight. Small motorhomes (25-30 feet) work perfectly fine on flooded acid batteries.

### Finding the Right Size Battery

▶ Estimate the amount of boondocking (no outside power source) on your itinerary.

▶ Consider whether adding more solar panels is in the near future.

▶ Check to see how much room is available in the outside basement or under the entrance steps in the motorhome to store and hook up these batteries, in case you want more.

▶ Replace a group 24 battery with a group 27 or even a group 29, which are physically larger (and heavier), providing more power over a longer period.

**Tip**: Check the top of the battery for a "group" number.

Overcharging and undercharging are the main reasons batteries deteriorate, but not keeping the cell water level constant is also a contributing factor.

Having an *Inverter* wired into the system eliminates the charging issues, and there are automatic systems available to handle keeping the cell water level in balance. It is still up to you to add the water.

**Note**: Before deciding how many batteries are required, keep in mind that the microwave /convection oven and the toaster oven do not generally operate without a good park electrical power source or a generator.

It takes 1500 watts of capacity to run the average microwave. *Ergo*, there is no point to four batteries if two is all you need.

Here are a few website links that provide detailed information to help you make a choice.

> www.**rv-batteries.com/about.php**
>
> blog.**woodalls.com/2010/03/rv-batteries-099-by-professor95/**
>
> www.**smithae.com/rv.html**

# Battery Maintenance

If your batteries are new: On your maintenance calendar, every 3 months, mark down "check battery water." If the batteries are several years old, check every month. Remember our motto, "take care of your vehicle, and it takes care of you;" this is certainly true for batteries.

Always use *Distilled Water* to replace the fluid inside the cells. I use a large eyedropper for control to ensure that no overfilling occurs. Enough air space must remain at the top of the cell so expansion can take place, if necessary.

The circles on the battery top shown here mark the cell covers. Gently pry them up with a non-metallic tool. Fill the cells to ⅛" below the fill well. Ensure the cover is re-seated firmly; I usually tap the cover a few times.

Do Not Overfill!

If your batteries do not have removable cell covers, they are sealed batteries and there is no maintenance required.

In a new, fully charged battery (less than a year old), no more than a few large eyedroppers full of water is usually needed for each cell. Sometimes no water is required. Add water to ⅛" below the bottom of the fill well.

With regular maintenance, if you find cells requiring a lot of water, it is possible that the battery needs replaced soon. To my surprise, flooded acid batteries have about a three-year life span.

Until the battery replacement, change the maintenance calendar reminder to every two weeks. You do not want the battery to boil over and become a possible fire hazard.

**Note**: If the battery is discharged, add water to a level just above the plates. This allows for expansion while charging.

To clean acid residue on the terminals, batteries, or the battery bracket, use a solution of baking soda and water. Purchase a special protection spray for the terminals to prevent corrosion, available at any auto store.

Once battery acid spills over, it continues to eat away at any metal it touches. Always clean the battery bracket before inserting the new batteries.

Tighten the terminals properly; terminals that are too tight or too loose could result in post breakage, meltdown or fire.

**Important**: Some batteries, when the cells run dry, are a fire hazard. Keep flames, sparks or metal objects away from the batteries at all times.

## Solar Panel for Battery Charging

To keep a balanced charge to your engine and/or coach batteries, adding a small solar panel may be the solution. For detailed information, visit:

**http://www.outsidesupply.com/rv-solar-guide/**

# The Basics of Solar Technology

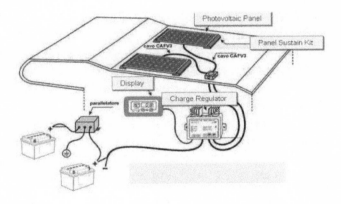

This is a costly addition but may repay the investment in one year if it enables you to boondock often. With commercial park rates soaring higher every year, the $500- $3,000+ cost for parts and installation may prove to be a good investment for some travelers.

Enjoying the beauty and solitude that nature offers, versus staring out at a paved parking lot, this may be incentive enough to justify the cost.

Solar panels (or modules) are categorized into three types, single crystal, multicrystalline, and amorphous. These refer to the type of surface that is sandwiched between, usually glass, and a type of thin encapsulation on the back.

▶ The single crystal solar panel, known to be the oldest and most efficient of the solar technologies, translates approximately 15 to 18% of the sun's light into electricity.

▶ The multicrystalline or polycrystalline panels use chips sliced from single crystals. Multicrystalline panels translate approximately 14% of the sun's light into electricity.

▶ The amorphous panels, made by sending an aluminum substrate through a vacuum chamber and blowing on the silicon gas, are the least efficient at 6-8%; probably not the best choice.

▶ You can identify most single crystal panels by their solid one color solar cells, the multicrystalline by their cells that are chip like and the amorphous which is usually brown and one complete surface.

For an RV, where space is at a premium, the single crystalline can deliver the maximum power in the smallest package. The multicrystalline is not quite as small as the single crystalline, but has the advantage of usually being a little less expensive.

The amorphous panel can take up double the space of a single crystalline to provide the same power and is the cheapest of these choices.

The amount of charging power a solar panel puts out is directly proportional to the intensity of the sunlight falling on it.

▶ Decrease the level of sunlight to half that of a bright sunny day; the charging power is reduced by half.

▶ Park your RV in a dusty parking lot for a few days and the panel output reduces.

▶ Heat also negatively affects the output of solar electric panels. Contrary to public perception, solar electric panels run off the sun's light not heat. In fact, the hotter the panel, or the more exact the cell gets, the less efficient it is.

▶ The most efficient place for solar electricity is up in space or in the high mountains where it is clean, clear and cold.

## Rating Solar Panels

All solar panels have a detailed energy label on the back. Generally, you can find the watts, volts and amps. This allows you to compare panels.

For the layperson, the watts are described as Nominal Peak Power (P max), the voltage as Peak Power Voltage (Vmp) and the amps as Peak Power Current (Imp). These are the conditions the solar panel can experience when hooked up to the battery.

# Quality of Solar Panels

Most solar panels come with 10-20 year warranties. It is extremely difficult to break a solar panel even though most are covered in glass. The panels pass extreme tests where lead balls are fired at the glass cover.

## Basic Requirements for Panels

▷ Look for panels that are 17 volts or higher. This voltage allows for enough voltage drop to be able to hit the batteries at the target of 14.2 volts.

▷ Identify a 17-volt panel by looking at the front of the solar panel and counting 36 cells. As each cell is just under one-half of a volt and tied together, a **36-cell panel** generally means it is at least 17 volts.

▷ A **30 or 33 cell panel** does not belong on the roof of an RV for true solar charging.

# Controllers

A charge controller (or regulator) sits between the solar panel and the batteries. The term "regulator" is really the best label. Its job is to regulate the flow of the electricity from the solar panels to the batteries.

▷ They protect the batteries from being overcharged by regulating the solar energy.

▷ Most units have a blocking diode or a one-way gate that does not allow your battery energy to flow out through the solar panel at night.

Conquer the Road: RV Maintenance for Travelers

▶ Many units have meters that show the amps coming from the solar panel and the voltage of
  the battery.

▶ Some units use just an LED that flashes when the
  battery is near full charge.

# Basic Regulating Technologies

### Shunt and Pulse Width Modulation

**Shunt type** technology has been around for quite a while.
Basically, electronic circuitry in the regulator measures battery voltage. As voltage increases to some preset number,
the solar energy is switched off or diverted, stopping the
flow of solar energy to the battery. When the charging stops,
the battery starts to fall. At some resumption set point,
charging resumes.

The draw back with the shunt type of controller is that it is
either on or off. When the preset reconnect voltage is
reached, it dumps all the available energy from the solar into
the battery. This can boil water out of your batteries. While
this type of controller is a low cost option, newer technologies have been proven to be nicer to your batteries.

**Pulse Width Modulation** (PWM) is now very standard as
the best you can get at an affordable price. PWM, pioneered
by Heliotrope General, has been proven by Sandia National
Labs to keep your batteries at the highest state of charge
with the least amount of water consumption.

▷ Initially during the day, all of the solar energy goes directly to the battery. After reaching a preset voltage, a PWM Taper Charge begins. The preset battery voltage is maintained by frequently switching the solar energy source on and off.

▷ After the preset voltage is reached and stabilized by the PWM, a float (trickle) charge holds the battery at the preset voltage.

▷ This strategy is just a bit more sophisticated and maximizes solar energy gain, keeping the batteries at their highest state of charge with the least amount of water consumption.

## Temperature Compensation

Achieve temperature compensation by running a wire from the controller to the batteries. At the end of the temperature compensation line is a probe that reacts to the temperature. This reaction is then sensed by the controller and changes the solar charging voltage.

# Inverter

An **Inverter** is an electronic device that converts battery power into a form that mimics conventional electric power. The most commonly purchased models produce a "modified square wave."

Premium inverters produce a "pure sine wave" to imitate grid power. This eliminates background noise so that all appliances, including electronics, work without anomalies.

They are particularly suited for sensitive electronics found in some desktop computers and high-quality sound equipment. This type of inverter is expensive, so most of us use the "modified wave" type.

The inverter in your RV does three jobs:

 ▶ Converts the battery power (DC) to AC when not plugged into an outside power source
 ▶ Directs DC power to the coach

▶ Charges the batteries properly, no overcharge or undercharge

All newer Class A coaches should come equipped with an inverter/charger. Check this before purchasing any RV, particularly a Class C or fifth wheel. To add an inverter is an expensive project.

Keep in mind that the microwave/convection oven and toaster oven generally do not run on battery power only. When boondocking these appliances are not available for use, so a smaller, less expensive inverter works fine.

It takes a 2800-watt inverter to run these energy-hungry appliances and a pure sine-type inverter to run them efficiently. Some research may be required here.

There are two ways to use the inverter:

▶ Leave the inverter on all the time and use it as a power backup when electrical glitches in the RV park system cause a brief shut-down. It also keeps the batteries charged at the proper rate, no overcharge or undercharge.

▶ Turn it on only when boondocking. Running the engine or generator works as a charger through the inverter.

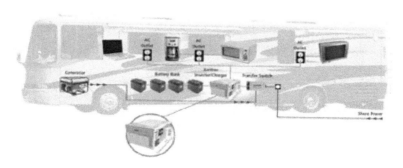

# Converter

If your RV does not have an inverter installed, then it has a converter. The converter's job, unlike the inverter, is to change 120 volts AC to 12 volt DC to supply power to all of the 12-volt appliances and accessories in the RV.

When not plugged into an outside electrical source, your coach batteries supply the power to all of the 12-volt appliances and accessories in the RV.

The converter's built-in battery charger works to keep the house batteries topped off with a trickle charge.

Older RV charger/converters generally charge at a fixed voltage in the range of 13.5 volts. This causes the boiling over problems that diminish the life of the coach batteries.

Fully charged coach batteries can be too much for a float charge, and over time, depletes the water level in the battery cells.

This is why it is important to check the water level in your batteries on a regular basis. Mark it on your calendar.

Along with the converter, at least a three-stage charger should be installed that can provide a bulk charge then an absorption charge and finally a float charge. Newer RV converters on the market are capable of charging the batteries in this way.

The converter/charger shown here has a 3-phase charger at about half the price of an inverter. If you stay connected to park power all the time and have no sensitive computer or stereo equipment, this looks like a good buy.

Find the documentation on your charger (try an online search) and determine if it has the newer 3-stage charger. Always keep a close eye on the water level in the batteries.

*See the diagram on the next page.*

The charger is probably located near the electric cable in an outside cabinet.

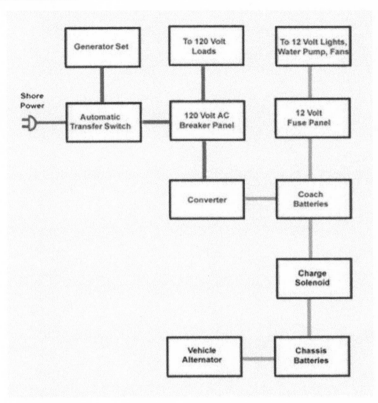

# Notes:

# Generator

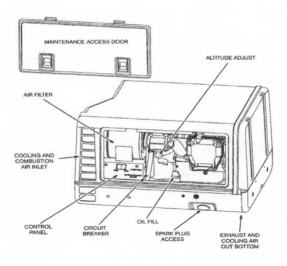

A generator supplies your coach with electricity to run all your lights and appliances as if connected to an outside electric source. Generally, it draws its fuel from the gas or diesel tank that supplies the engine.

Some RVs have a much larger propane tank that also supplies the generator along with the furnace, stove and hot water heater.

If you are planning to stay more than two nights in sites without electric hookups *(called boondocking)*, a generator is a necessity. Some travelers like to stay in out-of-the-way places to enjoy the desert, lakes and beaches that are easily accessible but do not provide utilities.

In order to keep your coach and engine batteries charged, run the generator at least once each day.

Before you leave on your first trip, have the generator serviced by a RV mechanic that specializes in generator maintenance. The oil/filter may need to be changed and the spark plugs checked and/or replaced.

**Important**: Before turning OFF the generator, ensure that the air conditioner is already OFF. The same applies when you turn the generator ON. This sudden shift in voltage sucks oil into the combustion chamber of the generator and fouls the plugs.

# Maintenance Procedures

When not using the generator, regular maintenance is required. To keep it running smoothly, ensure that it is run *no less than 30 minutes once a month*. This can be difficult due to the noise and fumes that could irritate other guests in a residential park.

Check with the park office for the appropriate hours to handle this chore. Running the generator during a *rest stop* along your travel path is also a good place to handle this procedure. Take a lunch break and enjoy the air conditioner.

Even if you store your RV more than one month, continue this maintenance schedule. Adding a fuel conditioner to the gas/diesel tank might help to extend the maintenance beyond the one-month requirement.

What happens if you do not keep up the maintenance? The generator stops working just when you need it the most. A costly repair replacing the carburetor may also ensue.

> ▶ Every 50 hours, change the oil and filter. It takes about 3 quarts of oil. Change the spark plugs too as part of the maintenance procedure.

> ▶ If spending time near ocean areas where salt water creates corrosion, do the maintenance procedure more often.

> ▶ If there is some difficulty starting the generator, spray contact lubricant into the carburetor.

Generators are designed to last for a long time when properly maintained.

Download the free "Gas *Onan Maintenance Schedule*" http://**RVMaintenance.MovingOnWithMargo.com**

---◆---

# Sewer System

There are a few things to know about an RV sewer system. Knowing what equipment to use and the best routine for dumping the tanks are the most important.

## Sewer Hose

 If you buy a used RV, it probably already has several sewer hoses and connectors. You may find, however, that they have reached their end-of-life. When purchasing new sewer hoses, purchase the *Rino Heavy-Duty* kit (or something similar) and another 5- or 10-foot extension of the same brand.

This hose is made of tougher and more flexible material. It has a built-in adapter for the RV connection and a seal for the park sewer connection, a very clean and neat solution.

Add the extension when the sewer connection is more than 15 feet from your RV.

There are also times when the park sewer opening is less than ten feet from the RV connection.

For a shorter hose, use just the extension. Switch out the park sewer end from the original 15-foot hose. (Look on the hose for the correct direction to twist the release to swap out the part.)

Purchasing the same brand for both hoses is essential for an easy swap out or extension.

*Rino* also makes a less-expensive 15-foot kit that is easier to store because the fabric is lighter weight and collapses down into a smaller space. That very design also makes it more susceptible to leaks from dragging it over the ground.

However, if you purchase some type of support device for the hose, this easier-to-store version works great. Keep the sewer hose off the ground and the problems disappear.

Sewer spillage is a very big no-no with state health departments and strictly enforced.

When buying the new sewer hose kit, also pick up a "sewer donut." In most states you do not need it, but occasionally a certain county regulation requires it.

Very inexpensive, it looks like a rubber donut  with one side elongated and narrower than the other side.

Squeeze it into any park sewer receptacle and it makes a generic fit for any sewer hose fitting. Some parks do not let you hook up to their sewer without it.

# Tips For A Happy Toilet

For the best smelling results (no smell) in the bathroom, keep it simple. Do not flush toilet paper, even the expensive RV type.

Store the toilet paper in a lidded container nearby. This keeps paper from fouling the sensors in the black water tank or creating a blockage that is hard to clear. Paper also creates its own smell that takes a long time to break down in the black water tank.

## Emptying the Gray and Black Water Tanks

1. Remove the protective cap that covers the sewer connection and attach the sewer hose. (See the photo below.) Make sure the RV connection end is securely fastened onto the corresponding notches.

2. **Slowly open ONLY the black water tank valve an inch or so.** Check for leaks at the connection points. If none, then fully open the tank valve. Wait a few moments to ensure the tank is empty, and then **close the valve**.

3. Next, pull the gray water valve and leave it open, unless you are moving on. This rinses the black water from the hose and avoids a mess when storing the hose for travel.

4.  Leave the gray water valve open until just before the next black water dump. This eliminates the need for frequent dumps of the gray water tank to keep it from overflowing into the shower/tub.

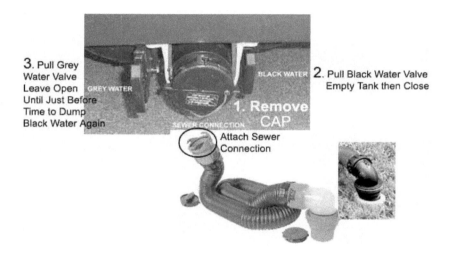

3. Pull Grey Water Valve Leave Open Until Just Before Time to Dump Black Water Again

GREY WATER

BLACK WATER 2. Pull Black Water Valve Empty Tank then Close

1. Remove CAP

SEWER CONNECTION

Attach Sewer Connection

**Important**: Replace the cap when traveling to your next destination. Some states may cite you for traveling down the road with liquid dripping from the sewer pipe.

## Routine Tank-dumping Procedure

1. After the black water tank is empty (and the outside valve closed), pour one capful of laundry detergent (scent-free) into the toilet. Allow a little water to flow in with the detergent. Continue to follow this procedure after each black water tank dump.

2. Leave the outside **gray water** tank valve **open** until you see on the inside gauge (or smell) the need to drain the black water tank.

   This eliminates dumping the gray water frequently and prevents backups into the shower. It is wise to keep a calendar of dump dates for a while until it becomes routine. The inside monitor gauge is rarely accurate unless the RV is less than 5 years old.

   **Important**: Always keep the outside **black water** tank valve **closed** between dumps. Liquid needs to build up to keep the contents from forming hard clumps and creating a clogged drain.

3. If you frequently smell odor from the tank, check the outside valve for a leak. Valve replacement may be necessary every ten years or so as the rubber seal disintegrates.

   Check the park office for a vendor recommendation or do it yourself. Pick up replacement parts at any Wal-Mart store.

4. Close the outside gray water valve a couple of days before the black water tank is ready to dump.

   *Just a heads up:* It may take two days to store enough water to flush the sewer hose after the black water dump. To flush properly, a rapid gush of gray water is required.

5. Remember to add one capful of scent-free laundry detergent to the toilet before pulling the outside black water valve.

6. The electronic sensor lights on the inside control panel are not very reliable, so only use them as a heads-up. It seems logical that the sensors located higher in the tank would be more accurate, but be cautious.

7. If the RV is 5 years old or newer, add a capful of liquid (or powder) Calgon Water Softener (Wal-Mart carries this) to the tank along with the laundry detergent.

   This keeps the sensors free of water deposits and improves sensor accuracy. Older RV tank sensors (depending on the amount of prior maintenance) may not be restored to accuracy by any method.

**Caution:** Remember, the gray water valve is closed just prior to the dump cycle. If you see the shower/tub fill with gray water from below, it is past time to empty the tanks.

**RO Alert**: If a Reverse Osmosis water filter system is installed, it continually adds water to the gray water tank until the pressurized storage tank is full. **This can add ten gallons or more to the gray water tank.**

If you leave the RV unattended for a few days, while still connected to the outside water source, **remember to open the gray water valve** to avoid a backup.

## Black Water Tank Maintenance

On your first outing with your RV, clean the black water tank using a wand inserted into the toilet from inside. You can purchase these at any RV store (or Wal-Mart).

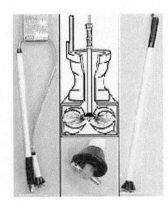

Basically, a cleaning wand is a piece of PVC pipe with a rotating cap for circulating the water on one end and a hose connector on the other end.

Two models shown here, one has a flex wand, the other a straight wand.

Turn off the outside water. Feeding your hose through a window, attach your water hose to this wand and insert it down into the tank.

Turn on the outside water and rotate the wand often. It may take 5-10 minutes of fairly high water pressure to clean the tank thoroughly.

**Tip 1**: To keep from dragging the water hose in through a window, purchase a *Water Bandit*, a rubber attachment that fits over the bathroom faucet.

One end of the *Bandit* has a regular male hose end. Attach a short hose to the wand; fit the rubber end over the bathroom faucet.

Turn on the water at the bathroom faucet, and you are in business. The *Water Bandit* is available at any hardware store.

**Tip 2**: Do not be tempted to pay a vendor to pressure-wash the black tank unless there is a serious clog. It takes a long time to build the bacteria back up that keeps the smell down.

Using the wand every six months works very well to keep the tank in balance, as long as you do not use toilet paper.

**New RV?** If the RV has less than 100 miles on the chassis, it is wise to start with some common black water tank enzymes for the first 2,000 miles. (*Happy Camper Holding Tank Treatment* recommended, especially in hot weather.) Use the **Routine Tank-dumping Procedure** above substituting the *Treatment* (available at Amazon) for the detergent.

## Gray Water Tank Maintenance

To keep odors out of the gray water tank, pour a cup of baking soda into the kitchen sink drain every few months.

My solution is to keep a small box of baking soda in my refrigerator to absorb odors there. After a few months, I toss the baking soda down the kitchen drain (after using it to scrub the sink), followed by plenty of water. This is called "practical recycling."

Place a stainless steel fine mesh strainer-type cover in the drain opening to catch the food particles that contribute to the odor.

There are also several products on the market that target the gray water tank. *Happy Camper* recommended for the black water tank works well for this purpose too.

# Notes:

# Propane Tank

Checking for propane leaks should be a top priority before purchasing any RV. Most RV repair services carry a simple vacuum tool that attaches to the stovetop. If a leak exists, the vacuum is broken.

When you take your RV out of storage, this test should be part of the pre-trip maintenance.

To turn off the propane for any reason, find the large valve handle similar to the one shown here. Turn the knob to the right just as if you were turning off water (*see photo, turnoff valve inside black circle*).

Propane does not degrade or create a hazard when sitting unused. The tank can be turned on again if necessary without calling a repairperson to make adjustments.

If the propane tank is turned on, and is almost empty, a distinctive odor similar to "rotten eggs" seeps into the interior of the RV.

This odor is added intentionally (federal regulation) to warn you it is time to fill up. The smell could also be a leak warning. Propane itself has no smell.

# Hot Water Heater

Unless you have the new "instant on," keeping this little hot water heater working properly can be a challenge.

Propane gas is the normal fuel that feeds it, igniting through a small tube.

The design itself is part of the problem, but the heater products remain the same. Eventually instant-on heaters will be standard.

## Use Electric Only or Combination

Usually fueled by propane only, some newer RV water heaters are equipped with both propane and electric options.

If you do not have a dual heater, with the high price of propane, adding an electric element (Lightning Rod) to the hot water heater may be more efficient.

Nightly and weekly rates at an RV park usually include the cost of electricity. Monthly stays where you pay the electric bill, the Lightning Rod element does add to the cost.

In the *pre-purchase inspection,* check the propane system for leaks. If you skipped this important item, have it checked now for later use when you may really need propane to run the furnace in sub-zero temperatures.

Most RV repair people have a simple vacuum tool that attaches to the stovetop propane source. If there are no breaks in the vacuum gage, there are no leaks.

## Troubleshooting the Water Heater

### What is that Noise?

When the noise is coming from the propane burner, it could be that the air-mixing gate is turned wrong. This is the where the gas enters the burner tube. *(See photo above.)*

The burner tube brings in air to stir with the propane. If it is not pulling in air properly, a noise can sometimes be heard.

If not enough air is mixing with the propane, the flame is low and does not burn as hot. This can cause the water heater not to keep enough heated water in the tank.

Adjust the air intake until the noise stops.

### Heater Does Not Light

The jet that the propane comes through to be lit can sometimes get clogged. Using a pipe cleaner or other tool, clean out the jet.

If the pilot light is lit by an electronic connection, checking the wires could find a loose connection. Best practice is to call a local RV repairperson for this fix.

## Loud Roar and Exhaust Soot

When the water heater turns on, if you hear a loud roar and you see soot coming out of the exhaust, it is possible that some insect has found a new home. Open the outside door and check for nests.

Sometimes insects build nests inside the curved part of the burner tube. Clean out the burning tube with a pipe cleaner. The tube should burn clean and efficient.

If it is faulty, carbon dioxide can leak into the interior of the coach.

## Odor In The Water

If there is an odor in the water, then more than likely a bacteria has built up in the heater. To remove the odor, the tank needs to be drained and flushed out with a chlorine and water mixture. This kills the bacteria. *(See Flushing the Hot Water Heater.)*

When storing a tank for a long period of time, it is best if water is not left in the tank to decrease the chances of bacteria growing.

## No Hot Water Out of the Faucet

If there is no hot water coming out of the faucet but the tank is warm, this indicates that the heater is working. It is best to look for a reason hot water might be rerouted away from the faucet.

A water heater bypass can be the cause of this. A lot of RVs-- but not all--have a water heater bypass. Switch the valves to allow water to flow into the water heater.

Another reason might be that more than one faucet is on at the same time. The water heater system allows cold water to flow over to the hot water side if water is requested in a second location.

# Replacing the Anode Rod

One of the most important considerations in extending the life of your water heater is whether the anode rod is performing its job - **to divert corrosive action away from the tank walls to the anode rod**.

*New or Reborn    Needs replacing*

Salt water also shortens the life of the rod, so if you have a soft water conditioning system that uses salt, be prepared to replace the rod sooner.

When you smell an offensive odor in the water, it is time to flush the water heater.

Depending on the needs of the user, there are several options when making a selection.

If you have a *Suburban* brand of hot water heater, replacing your anode rod at regular intervals may **increase the life of your water heater**, saving you money, time and the inconvenience of having to replace your water heater.

*Atwood* manufactures a water heater with an aluminum tank that resists corrosion, hence no anode rod necessary. There are some older Atwoods, however, that need an anode rod. The only way to tell is to open the drain valve.

If there is a anode rod installed (not a heating element), then your water heater needs an anode rod replacement.

Magnesium, aluminum, or a combination of aluminum, zinc, and tin are the most common elements used to manufacture anode rods. There are also flexible options for low ceiling clearance or difficult access points.

The condition of your anode rod (and whether it is time to replace it) depends upon your water quality, how much the water heater is used, the running temperature, and of course the craftsmanship of the tank itself.

## Flushing the Hot Water Heater

This is a simple project, but it does require a wrench or other tool to remove the drain plug. To complete the flush, purchase a flushing tool (photo below) from any RV store.

To make sure you follow the steps in order, write everything down on a card. After the flush, store the card away for next time.

**Option**: Soak the tank in white vinegar to better release the mineral residue. Getting the vinegar into the tank through a small drain hole can be tricky. If you have help or a way to attach a long flexible funnel from the drain hole to, say, the awning arm, it might work for you. [Step-by-step Instructions follow on the next page.]

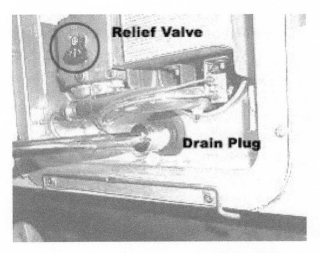

1. Turn off the water heater and allow several hours for it to cool.

2. Before you remove the drain plug, run some water from one of the hot faucets to make sure that the water is not hot enough to burn.

3. Cover the gas burner tube to protect it from the water draining out.

4. Turn off the water to the RV and remove the drain plug or electric element (*Lightning Rod* or *Hot Rod*).

5. To drain it more quickly, lift the lever of the pressure relief valve. That allows air into the heater and the tank drains much quicker; and it is good to exercise the valve to keep it working properly.

6. *With the drain plug out*, **close the relief valve** and turn city water back on to flush out the tank.

7. Install the flushing tool (shown here) to a garden hose and use it to wash the interior of the heater by pointing it downward.

   This ensures that all solids are flushed from the heater.

8. Continue to use the flushing tool until the water is clear. Once the water comes out clean, allow the water to drain, reinstall the drain plug or heating element, and refill the water heater.

9. Wrap the drain plug threads with Plumber's tape. To secure the drain plug against a possible link, again, ask your strong neighbor for help.

10. Once the heater is filled, run water through a hot water faucet to be sure the air is all out, then turn the heater back on.

11. Store the tools in a plastic bag to keep them clean until time to do this job again next year.

*Option*: To ensure all the mineral deposits are cleaned out of the tank, add 3 gallons of white vinegar to a 6-gallon tank and set soak for 2 hours minimum, then flush.

# Water Pump

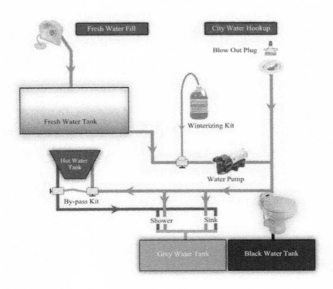

The RV water system consists of a fresh-water holding tank, plastic or copper water pipes, a 12 volt RV water pump, a gray water tank, a black water tank and a valve (or two) for dumping the waste.

 RV water pumps are relatively simple devices. Your RV's pump is probably made by Shurflo, the standard pump manufacturer. It is always powered by 12 volt DC electricity through the inverter, even if you are plugged into a 120 volt AC power.

The RV water pump is an "on demand" system. This means that the pump only kicks on when requested. They work by pressurizing your water pipes to a preset PSI (pounds per square inch).

This is usually about 30 PSI but most pumps are adjustable. When power is switched on to the pump, it starts pumping. If any faucets are open, the pump continues to run providing the necessary flow of water.

When you shut the faucet off, the pump continues to run until the preset water pressure is built up in the plumbing lines. When this pressure is reached, the pump automatically turns off.

The pressure in the line is maintained until you open a faucet again. When you open the faucet, the pump senses a drop in pressure and begins pumping again.

Some older RV water pumps require you to turn the pump on only when you want water. You open the faucet, turn the pump on and water flows out of the faucet. When you want to turn the water off, you turn the switch off to the pump and then close the faucet.

It is important to do things in this order. These older pumps do not shut off when the water reaches a preset pressure in the line. Leaving the pump running either overheats the pump or bursts a plumbing line.

## Pump Not Working

▶ Check the tank itself to be sure there is actually water in the fresh water holding tank. Believe it or not, this is often overlooked.

▶ It's possible for the water gauges to accumulate residue on them and read full when they are in fact empty.

▶ Make sure there is power to the pump. Is your RV battery fully charged? If not, you can plug into 120V power to make sure you have power to the pump.

▶ There is usually a fuse in the positive wire somewhere near the pump. Check the fuse to see if it is blown. If it is blown, replace it and your problem is solved.

▶ Check to see if the electrical connections to the pump are good. Use a 12 volt test light or better yet a multi-meter to check for power at the pump.

▶ If there are bad spots in the wiring, you need to repair or replace the wiring.

▶ The switch to the pump failed. Replacing this may be beyond your expertise, so find a local repair service.

▶ If the pump comes on but does not pump water, it is possible that the diaphragm in the pump has debris in it or it is punctured.

▶ Three screws attach the pump head to the pump casing. Remove these screws and inspect the rubber diaphragm.

If damaged, replace it with the repair kit that you can get from the manufacturer. You can usually buy these at your local RV parts dealer.

▶ If the diaphragm looks okay, clean it thoroughly with a gentle detergent and flush the pump head to remove any debris that may have entered it.

▶ Check to see that the supply line from the fresh water holding tank to the RV water pump is not blocked or punctured. Sometimes there is a shut off valve on this line. Make sure that it is open.

▶ If the line is blocked with debris or ice, you need to clear it somehow. Try disconnecting the line at the pump and blow compressed air through the pipe.

Be sure and turn the pressure down low on the compressor. You do not want to blow the line and cause a leak. If there is a leak in this supply line, it needs to be repaired or replaced.

▶ Check the connection at the inlet side of the pump to make sure it is not sucking air.

▶ If the pump does not shut off, there is a leak somewhere in the system. It is either at the outlet connection on the pump, in the plumbing, or at the faucet.

# Fresh Water Tank

There are only a few things to know about tanks. In freezing conditions, drain or use potable antifreeze to keep tanks from bursting. If your RV ever needs a replacement tank, however, it is best not to try to patch it.

It is a good idea to follow this sanitation procedure when you first purchase your RV, right before you take your first trip.

- Reserve 5 to 10 hours to complete the task
- Change the internal and external filters after you finish sanitizing the water system
- Flush out your hot water tank at the same time (see *Flushing the Hot Water Heater*)

Sanitize the water system at least once a year if boondocking frequently or storing for a season.

# Sanitizing the Fresh Water System

1. Drain all of the water out of the water system; this includes hot water tank, fresh water tank, and the water lines. Close all of the drain valves before continuing.

   You do not want to start this process with water that is questionable or of unknown quality in your RV water system.

2. Determine the size of your RV water system: the fresh water tank plus the hot water tank and 2 to 3 gallons for water lines depending on the size of your recreation vehicle.

3. Prepare a 5% solution using chlorine bleach (non-scented and non-gel) and water. Example: For a 60-gallon (227 liters) water tank, add 1.5 cups (360 ml) bleach to 6 gallons of water.

4. Add the bleach mixture to the water tank - *never pour straight bleach* into the RV fresh water tank as this destroys any gaskets along the way.

5. Top up the fresh water tank with water.

6. Run the chlorinated water through all lines (hot and cold one at a time) for one or two minutes. You should be able to smell the chlorine.

7. Top up the fresh water tank with water again.

8. Let it sit for 4 hours minimum, over night is best. The most important thing is to wait the appropriate amount of time for the tank to be properly sanitized.

9. Drain and rinse the water tank and water lines several times with fresh water.

10. To handle the chlorine smell and taste, add a mixture of 1/2 cup of baking soda and a gallon of water to the fresh water tank, repeat the fresh water flush.

Just in case you need to figure out how much water your fresh water tank really holds, here is the formula:

Length x Width x Height divided by 231 equals the Gallons of the Tank.

**LxWxH divided by 231 = Gallons**

# Notes:

# Refrigerator

Compared to a household refrigerator, an RV absorption re-frigerator cools much slower. The larger the refrigerator, the more efficient it is. The big plus to the absorption type, be-sides the "no moving parts," is the quiet operation.

Venting is required to remove the heat generated by the absorption process. A mechanical fan could handle the heat, but a fan proves impractical due to the battery drain and the noise level.

The manufacturing standard in most RVs today is a compli-cated absorption process. RV refrigerators operate by pre-cisely heating a sealed cooling element. The heating options are a gas flame, or an electric heating element.

However, custom-built models and some of the larger 40 ft.+ RVs install household refrigerators apparently without any issues in operation.

The cooling unit amounts to a series of tubes filled with an ammonia-based liquid.

As heat is applied, the fluid circulates through the cooling unit drawing the heat out of the refrigerator.

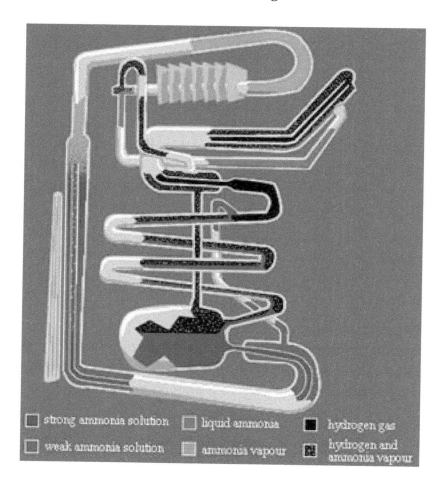

strong ammonia solution    liquid ammonia    hydrogen gas

weak ammonia solution    ammonia vapour    hydrogen and ammonia vapour

When an RV refrigerator starts failing (not cooling as well as it should), it means the fluid is no longer circulating properly through the cooling unit.

There are no moving parts. There are no pumps or compressors. When the ammonia is heated, it circulates. The freezing and cooling is accomplished simply by heating liquid and circulating it.

If the cooling unit develops a leak, the ammonia smell smacks you in the nose. This is not a very common occurrence. If it does happen, you immediately know where the problem is.

More often, the problem with an RV refrigerator is time combined with lack of use.

As RV refrigerators age, the ammonia liquid can create sediment that settles to the bottom of the cooling unit. This sediment impedes the ability of the ammonia to circulate properly through the cooling unit. As the sediment builds up, the refrigerator cools less and less.

A refrigerator that is used once or twice a year over a period of 5 or 6 years is much more likely to plug up than one that is in continual operation.

Fluid movement keeps any sediment suspended in the fluid, which ultimately prevents any accumulation from occurring.

# Things You Can Do to Keep It Cool

## Level the Refrigerator

The RV must be fairly level for the refrigerator to operate properly. Older RV refrigerators required more precise leveling, but even newer models must be close to level for optimum performance.

Over time, a cooling unit operated out of level is permanently damaged. Purchase a small bullseye level and place it in the freezer when leveling the RV.

Traveling with the refrigerator operating does not cause problems because the liquids and gases in the cooling unit are constantly moving around.

They do not collect and stay in areas of the cooling unit as in a stationary, out of level refrigerator.

## Pre-cool the Refrigerator

Turn the refrigerator on the day before you plan to leave. When you put in the food, make sure it is already cold. Frozen food should already be frozen.

Putting cold food in the refrigerator, rather than adding warm food, makes less work for the refrigerator. Avoid over packing a refrigerator. There must be space between the foods to allow air to circulate throughout the compartment.

Keep a thermometer in the freezer compartment and one in the refrigeration compartment. Check the thermometers frequently to ensure the freezer stays at zero degrees and the refrigerator stays below 40 degrees.

These temperatures may not be possible to sustain in heat over 100 degrees, so be prepared to check food for spoilage. Installing a vent flue fan helps with this issue. (See *Exterior Flue Fans.*)

### Interior Refrigerator Fan

To assist with air circulation, purchase an inexpensive, battery-operated refrigerator fan. Place the fan in the front of the refrigerator compartment.

It improves the efficiency by circulating the air and reduces the initial cool down time by half.

Two Alkaline size "D" batteries can last about two or three months. This fan is well worth the battery expense as it keeps food much fresher, especially salad greens, and reduces the moisture buildup.

Put this on your maintenance calendar to check every two months.

Recommended            Second choice

**Exterior Flue Fans**

If your travel plans include an extended stay in a very hot climate (over 90 degrees F daily), the refrigerator may not stay cool enough to keep food fresh.

Installing a couple of 12 V computer case fans at the top of the refrigerator flue vent eliminates this problem. Depending on the size of your RV refrigerator flue, there may only be room for one large fan.

Some refrigerator designs may require the fan to be installed at the bottom. Avoid this if possible.

Some service installers may spin a tale about the best installation, but I have tried both top and bottom vent placement. The fans installed in the top of the vent far outperform the bottom location.

The top vent design is a tougher install project and may cost a few more dollars in labor, but well worth it when the temperature hits 110 degrees. If you understand 12V schematics, it is an easy installation.

Measure the top surface opening of the refrigerator flue. Purchase these small computer case fans at a local electron-
ics/computer store or online (about $5 each
on Amazon).

Do it yourself or contact a local RV repairperson to install the fans at your RV park site.

Install an on/off switch within easy reach for flexibility in colder climates.

**Caution**: Do not allow the RV repairperson to purchase the fans. They do not usually have the correct specifications or understand the reasoning behind using computer case fans over conventional refrigerator vent fans. Computer fans are also less expensive ($5 versus $35).

**Note**: Unless your RV is less than 20 feet long, ignore the solar-type vent fans, as they do not produce enough airflow to do the job.

*Minimum specifications to ensure high airflow and low fan noise:*

**120 mm** (5 inch) **Computer Case Fan**:
Air Flow (FM) 44.03; Max. Noise dBA) 23.5

**80 mm** (3 inch) **Computer Case Fan**:
Air Flow (CFM) 28.89; Max Noise (dBA) 20.9

# Routine Refrigerator Maintenance

The heat created by the cooling process is vented behind the refrigerator. Air enters through the outside lower refrigerator vent and helps to draft the hot air out through the roof vent.

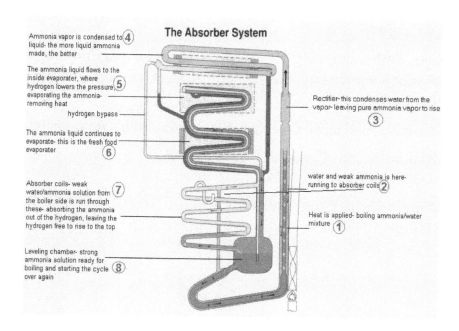

The Absorber System

Ammonia vapor is condensed to (4) liquid- the more liquid ammonia made, the better

The ammonia liquid flows to the inside evaporater, where hydrogen lowers the pressure (5) evaporating the ammonia- removing heat

hydrogen bypass

The ammonia liquid continues to evaporate- this is the fresh food evaporater (6)

Absorber coils- weak water/ammonia solution from (7) the boiler side is run through these- absorbing the ammonia out of the hydrogen, leaving the hydrogen free to rise to the top

Leveling chamber- strong ammonia solution ready for boiling and starting the cycle (8) over again

Rectifier- this condenses water from the vapor- leaving pure ammonia vapor to rise (3)

water and weak ammonia is here- running to absorber coils (2)

Heat is applied- boiling ammonia/water mixture (1)

> ▷ Periodically inspect the back of the refrigerator and the roof vent for any obstructions like bird nests, leaves or other debris that might prevent the heat from escaping.

> ▷ Remove the outside lower vent cover to access the back of the refrigerator. With the refrigerator turned off, ensure all connections are clean and tight.

- Turn the refrigerator on in the LP gas mode and look at the flame. Is it is burning poorly, or yellow-colored? Is the refrigerator not operating properly in the gas mode? It is possible that the baffle inside the flue is covered with soot.

- Clean the burner assembly (Liquid Heat Exchanger area) with a pipe cleaner.

- Turn the refrigerator off again and locate the burner. Directly above the burner is the flue. The baffle is inside the flue. Wear a pair of safety glasses and use an air compressor to blow air up into the flue.

- After the flue is clean, use compressed air to remove any debris from the outside compartment.

- Turn the refrigerator on in the LP gas mode to make sure it is working properly. Look for the bright blue flame, a sign everything is operating properly.

Road vibrations loosen deposits allowing them to crumble and fall to the burner below. The finer particles fall into the burner itself, while the larger pieces remain on top of the burner and cause problems with the flame sensor.

As the fine particles build up inside the burner, they create problems with the flame and reduce the heat output of the burner.

Pull out the orifice and soak it in some rubbing alcohol, then allow it to air dry. If you cannot get it clean, just replace it, not the whole refrigerator or cooling unit! For a thorough cleaning of the flue and baffle, it may necessary to have an RV dealer do it for you. Schedule an LP gas pressure test too.

# Refrigerator Not Working

There are a number of reasons that a refrigerator does not function; typically, those problems can be repaired at a reasonable cost.

## Propane Gas Does Not Ignite

This sounds silly, but check to ensure that the outside propane tank is turned ON. Simple solutions are the best solutions.

## Pilot Light

If the pilot light does not stay lit, you may have a bad thermocouple that controls gas flow.

## Electronic Ignition

If your electronic ignition fails to light, you may have a faulty control board.

## Works on Gas Only

If your refrigerator works on gas, but does not work on electric, you may have a burned out heating element.

If any of these problems exist for you, have a qualified technician check it. This is not something you can fix without experience in this field.

A word to the wise, if the problem lies in the cooling unit, you may be better off buying a new RV refrigerator instead of repairing your old one.

The high cost of repair is the labor taking the old refrigerator out, taking it apart and putting it back together, then re-installing it; usually an all day job. Install a new one in about an hour.

Take some time and check out the pricing before committing to a repair.

## Absorber Cool, Boiler Section Hot

If your refrigerator is not staying cool, check the absorber. Is it cool, and the boiler section hot? (See *Routine Refrigerator Maintenance* for a diagram of the unit.)

This is relatively easy to check, but to get the most accurate reading of the cooler temperature, stick a thermometer in a glass of water (necessary to equalize the temperature) and put it in the refrigerator.

After 12 hours, the temperature should be no higher than 43 degrees F. After 24 hours, it should be in the low 20s to high 30s maximum.

If you cannot maintain these temperatures, the cooling unit is bad. Rebuild the unit, or replace the entire refrigerator. If this is happening in very hot weather, read the *Exterior Flue Fans* section before making a decision.

First, check the level of the refrigerator. Propane-style refrig-erators must be level, and if they are not, they do not work. This is the easy solution, and it could save you a lot of money.

# Boondocking Tips

If you boondock a lot you may be interested to know how much propane your refrigerator uses. As discussed earlier, it is important to keep an eye on the monitor, or the manual gauge on the outside tank.

If you have a 12 cu/ft Norcold refrigerator that burns 2400 BTU/hr., one gallon of propane lasts about 38 hrs. However, that applies only if the refrigerator runs constantly. Again, assuming it runs for 8 hours out of a 24 hr. period, a gallon of propane lasts about 5 days.

It all depends on how hot the outside temperature is; how full the refrigerator is; the temperature setting and how often you open the door. If you have a 30-gallon propane tank, it should last about 150 days.

## Climate Control Drains Battery

Some refrigerators have a "high humidity" switch, or equivalent. This is usually located in the freezer doorframe and attaches to a small heater element. It controls the humidity that may collect around the door opening during very high humidity situations.

This circuit draws about 6 amps and drains a battery in less than 12 hours. This is an easy solution. Flip the switch to the "off" position when running the refrigerator on battery power.

# Furnace

Since I never leave the Sunbelt, my furnace has never been used. A small space heater takes care of the morning and evening chill.

However, many travelers seem destined to wind up in cold places, not always by choice. The furnace becomes an important part of their lives. It is noisy, burns lots of propane, and generates soot.

If it is not working, however, the scenario can be life threatening. It is wise to understand the basics.

- ▶ **What is a BTU?** 1 BTU equals the heat energy required to raise the temperature of 1 pound of water by 1 degree F. To calculate the BTU rating: Total sq. ft. of RV x 125 = BTU needed.

- ▶ The RV furnace fan is powered by the 12VDC system. Even when boondocking, the furnace ignites and burns through propane at a rapid rate, cycling on and off with the thermostat.

▶ After turning on the furnace, wait for about 15 to 30 seconds for the furnace blower to start. This is usually a very loud sound, so be prepared. The air coming from the blower is cold at this point.

▶ The burner ignites after the blower starts.

▶ Because of the thermostat, the blower and burner cycle on and off depending on the temperature setting. The burner shuts down first, with the blower some seconds later.

▶ Five gallons of propane (20 lb. tank) should last for roughly 18 hours. A furnace with a rating of 26,000 BTUH consumes 1 gallon of liquid propane every 3.5 hours.

**11** **DC Wiring Diagram**

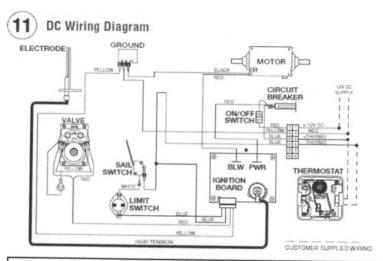

IMPORTANT: If any original wire has to be replaced, it must be replaced with type 105 C or its equivalent. Terminal Block on 85 Models only.

# Furnace Not Working or Operating Correctly

▷ If your furnace refuses to operate, the first thing to check is the wall mounted thermostat switch.

▷ Ensure that the ON/OFF switch is in the ON position. I know, this seems silly, but this is a frequent occurrence according to a survey of mobile repair services.

▷ There is a furnace vent located on one side of the RV. If there are problems running the furnace, look for a wasp nest inside the vent.

At any RV supply store, purchase a little screen designed to eliminate this problem. **If your RV is still under warranty, wait before adding this little screen set. This may void the warranty since it is not recommended by the manufacturer.**

▷ Mice and other critters can also build nests inside. Check for debris as cooler weather approaches. If your rig is stored in a grassy field, make periodic checks for signs of rodents.

▷ A rumor circulating the RV communities is that placing LED rope lights around the bottom of the RV keeps critters out. You might try this. This does mean leaving them on 24x7.

▷ If the gas pressure is not at 11.00 W.C., the furnace works inconsistently and creates an unbalanced combustion. Get a qualified propane technician to complete a Manometer test to determine that the proper LPG pressure of 11.00 W.C. exists for furnace use.

▷ A simple pressure-drop test can determine if there is a gas leak. Any mobile repairperson can do this.

▷ Be careful not to cover or restrict the heater ducts. Pressure can back up and cause the furnace to malfunction.

- Check the air intake and flue areas of the furnace for obstructions caused by critter nests.

- Use a multimeter to test that the DC voltage is between 10.5 and 13.5 VDC at the furnace during operation. Low voltage can cause the furnace to overheat.

  Check the battery monitor for starting voltage. If the voltage is in the range, then the problem lies at the furnace.

- Check for a tripped circuit breaker. Check the "line monitor" first to ensure that the polarity is correct. (See *Managing Power*.)

- If the blower runs but fails to ignite, check the air intake for restrictions.

# Filtering Your Water

Almost every location in the USA suffers from polluted water. To stay healthy, *filter all water coming into* the RV.

## Exterior Water Filter

The best exterior water filter systems feature a sturdy house-quality canister (usually blue opaque) with a coarse filter to take out the heavy materials.

A carbon filter canister can be daisy-chained to the primary filter by using a brass male-to-male or female-to-female hose adapter.

These canisters are then connected to your drinking water hose that fastens to the main park water source on your site.

These filters do not remove anything but sediment and chlorine (if using the carbon filter too).

Hardware stores often carry this blue canister. Since it is designed for pipe water transfer, make sure you get the adapters for "pipe to hose." One male-to-female, and one female-to-male are necessary to hook up to the water hoses at your site. Two "for drinking water only" hoses are required (see *Drinking Water Hoses and Connectors*).

My experience is that the smaller white canisters usually found in the RV supply section are worthless, except, perhaps, to daisy chain a charcoal filter to the larger one.

## Drinking Water Filters

For drinking water, install a *Reverse Osmosis water filter system* under your kitchen sink cabinet, or under the dinette seat.

The Reverse Osmosis process eliminates bacteria, fluoride, and chlorine.

There are several designs available, but I recommend a two-gallon storage tank. This comes with a four-filter system: carbon, pre-filter, osmosis unit, and the small final filter to take out any storage tank taste or smell.

Order these systems online or through a local water store. Do the installation yourself, or find a park-recommended vendor by checking at the front desk.

The RO system is a fairly simply installation, you just need to ensure that the hoses are connected properly. No AC or DC power required.

It does require at least 40-psi water pressure (the standard for most RV parks).

You can purchase a water pressure hose gauge at your local hardware store, or online, if you have reason to doubt the park pressure level.

For complete information on how reverse-osmosis systems work, visit: *science.howstuffworks.com/reverse-osmosis.htm*

## Drinking Water Hoses and Connectors

Carry a male-to-male and a female-to-female drinking water hose adapter in the outside compartment where you keep the water hoses and gaskets.

Male-to-Male Adapter    Female-to-Female Adapter

Drinking Water Hose 5/8 inch

5/8 x 25 feet
5/8 x 10 feet
5/8 x 04 feet

Keep them in the bin with your 4-foot, 10-foot, and 25-foot drinking water hoses.

If you use the blue filter cartridge as mentioned in the *Exterior Water Filter* section, add the "pipe-to-hose" connectors as well.

Some park water connections are not standard, so be prepared. Include a small supply of different size hose gaskets to handle the connection leaks that occur without warning.

## Water Purity Tester

One tool I find very useful is a water purity tester. The *IntelliTEC Water Quality Tester* I purchased is more accurate that those expensive test strips. It is reasonable priced and has an off/on button and a "read" button so you can read the results after removing the tester.

Since it is digital, it reads instantly. *HM Digital* also makes a TDS meter that works well.

## Extra Cable

Bring 15 to 25 feet of extra RG6 cable as an extension for your high-definition flat-screen TV. It pays to be flexible.

Some RV parks may place their cable receptacle in hard to reach locations. If you plan on carrying a portable high-definition satellite TV dish with you, the extra cable may be necessary.

Include a couple of barrel connectors (small round adapters that connect two coaxial "F" connectors together) in this kit.

You may find that the original internal coaxial cable (probably RG58) in your RV does not make a good connection to your new high-definition flat screen TV.

Instead of having the entire RV rewired with RG6 (very expensive), run your extra cable through a window directly to the back of the TV.

Ensure that the pins, within the "F" connectors at each end, are inserted properly and tightened. Look for a bent pin in the connector if there is a problem.

# N otes:

———————◆———————

# Towing Your Car

To tow or not to tow is a major decision for most motorhome travelers. Take your first short trip without a tow in place, then make the decision.

The cost of fuel, the inconvenience of hooking and unhooking the tow, the lack of transportation at your destination, and road safety are the topics usually discussed on this issue. Lack of strength to lift the tow bar may also be an issue.

Not towing any vehicle behind the motorhome:

*Upside*:

- More flexibility for the driver
- No increased fuel cost

*Downside*:

- Hassle of finding a rental auto while at destination
- Limits exploration due to lack of transportation
- Hooking up and unhooking the towed car takes time and is sometimes frustrating

Most travelers find the convenience of having a touring car worth the inconvenience. You can then attach one of those cute little signs in the rear window of the car, "I'm a Toad," or "I'm Pushing As Fast As I Can," and other fun slogans.

*Without a tow car,* it is possible to hire someone in the RV park to shuttle you to the grocery store. However, if you like to explore museums and tourist attractions, this might get cumbersome. Try it without a tow for a trip, then decide.

In you are in a metro area, hiring a taxi is a viable option. Some parks actually have cars for hire.

If you choose the car option, ensure that your "toad" can travel "wheels-down." Wheels-down means that all four wheels touch the road while towing.

Install the heavy tow rig on the back of the motorhome, and a lightweight hookup receptacle on your car. Hooking it up takes about five minutes and can cause some frustration if traveling alone.

The expense of installing the tow equipment is approximately $1,000 for both vehicles. It is best to find an installer that is familiar with your car and towing hardware to get the best installation.

Some used motorhomes come with the tow equipment included. Autos can also be purchased already equipped to be towed. Look for these already rigged vehicles first.

Not every automobile can be towed wheels-down. Do your research on this. Your current auto may not be capable of being towed without a tow dolly.

Here are some websites to explore for information:

- *www.**trailerlife.com*** (lists of towable automobiles)
- *www.**escapees.com/*** Select **Discussions**. (*For Sale* section)
- *www.**rvforum.net*** (Discussions on towed autos)
- www.**blueox.us**/instruction/**towingbasics101**.htm

Pay close attention to the auto weight as well as the towability. If purchasing a high-powered diesel motorhome you can pull just about any weight. On the other hand, a small gas-powered motorhome has severe limitations on its pulling power.

Try to stay under 4,000 pounds if possible. Obviously going up and down hills or mountains can create a severe strain on the engine, hence the lighter weight. You may also need additional braking power.

Any tow vehicle is going to get some exterior damage from rocks and debris. When traveling I use a padded vinyl front cover for my Honda CR-V. It extends above the windshield and fastens to the doors and wheel wells.

It is time consuming to install and store so I do not usually expend the effort for short trips.

When towing be prepared to have a problem now and then detaching the car from the tow bar.

Best practice is to unhook on a flat straight surface. If you decide to unhook the toad while the motorhome is at an odd angle, the safety pins on the tow bar may jam.

# Notes

# Motorhome Tires

Since you are going to take the motorhome in for service be-fore you start on your first trip, ask the technician to check the tire pressure and note any bumps, checks, or slits in all four/six tires.

Have the technician find the "tire date" for you. Usually it is located in the embossed area where other information is stored. Sometimes it can be on the "inside" of the tire.

Write this date down on your *"My Motorhome Components"* sheet for future reference. Download this components sheet from my blog website:

*http://RVMaintenance.MovingOnWithMargo.com.*

When replacing tires, buy them all stamped with the same date code. This date should be as close to the purchase date as possible.

This ensures that they all came from the same manufacturing batch and should be evenly balanced on the road with lots of life left on the sidewalls.

Michelin recommends "any tires in service 10 years or more from the date of manufacture, including spare tires, be replaced with new tires as a simple precaution even if such tires appear serviceable and even if they have not reached the legal wear limit."

- If the cracks are less than 1/32" deep, the tire is O.K. to run.
- Between 1/32" and 2/32", the tire is suspect and should be examined by your tire dealer.
- If the cracks are over 2/32", the tire should be replaced immediately.

Wear bars, narrow strips of smooth rubber across the tread, appear when 2/32nd of an inch of tread remains. Replace the tire immediately.

Keeping proper tire pressure is one of best ways to help tires last longer. Follow the psi pressure listed on the tire itself.

The only portable air compressors small enough to travel with you do not have enough power to pump up a motorhome tire. Even those compressors that claim to have up to 120 psi rarely prove to be powerful enough.

That means relying on tire or repair shops. When taking the motorhome in for an oil change, insist that they check the tire for cuts, checks, and tread depth.

Find out the correct psi by looking directly on the tire and make sure they write it down on the order form.

The pressure psi listed on the tire is not a recommendation, but a maximum pressure that should not be exceeded at maximum load.

Recommended tire pressure is also displayed on the manufacturer's plaque on the driver side panel, or on inside the glove box door. I find, however, the psi recommended by the manufacturer is too low. It is better to find the psi listed on the tire and follow that recommendation.

After cleaning the motorhome tires with soap and water, apply a non-petroleum-based product like *303 Aerospace Protectant*. As far as I know, this is the only product that works as advertised in combating UV damage.

Another thing to consider is the fact that any tire dressing that contains petroleum products, alcohol, and/or silicone materials may further damage the tire due to a possible chemical reaction with the antioxidant material in the tire.

Most owners cover the tires when spending more than a few days in one location. There are vinyl covers available at any RV store.

However, it is a dirty job to cover and uncover the tires as the vinyl tends to pick up dirt and insects just like the tires. They can also blow off in heavy winds.

The latest tire cover option is shade cloth. The most effective way is to have snap or twist fasteners permanently installed around the wheel wells.

It is easy to remove and store the shade. Visit this vendor's product to see how it works, then find a local vendor to sell and install the shades: *http://www.rvsungard.com/tire-savers*

## Rotation and Alignment

The consensus among RV tire experts online is to rotate the tires only if you see irregular wear patterns on the front tires. This might also indicate an alignment is necessary.

Personally, I had an alignment done as soon as I bought my used motorhome, and the tires rotated according to my chassis manufacturer's instructions (important). My tires are wearing well to this day, several years later.

If you put 10,000 miles a year on your motorhome, the tires are probably going to be replaced before you need to have them rotated. Although, having an alignment done even with a new motorhome is a good idea; today's quality control is not rigorous.

# Hydraulic Leveling Systems

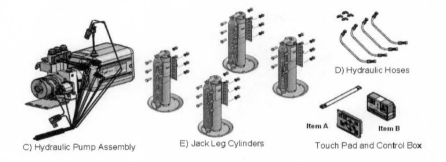

C) Hydraulic Pump Assembly     E) Jack Leg Cylinders     D) Hydraulic Hoses     Item A   Item B     Touch Pad and Control Box

Choosing a motorhome with a hydraulic leveling system eliminates the hassle of using leveling blocks under all the wheels. Since the refrigerator needs to be level to work properly, leveling becomes a priority when arriving at our destination, especially after dark.

When arriving at your destination, walk around the motorhome to determine the soil content. If it looks or feels soft, use leveling blocks under the jack pads.

This is especially important if the motorhome is over 32 feet and diesel-powered (heavy), as the pads can dig large holes in the ground.

The control panel is usually located next to the steering wheel in most cockpits.

When extending any of the jacks, a noisy bong sounds until shut off. When retracting, the bong continues until all jacks are safely docked.

Learn the shifting sounds of the bong to help determine the progress of the hydraulics.

# Maintenance Procedures

The hydraulics do require some maintenance.

- A careful maintenance check twice a year should be enough to keep the system running smoothly. Exercise the levelers, six times up and down, to lubricate them.

- If you notice that one or more of the levelers do not fully retract or extend, a full maintenance is suggested. Another problem might be that the level pad slips off its stanchion when extended onto a small rock.

- Check the reservoir with the jacks (and any slideout) in the **fully retracted** position. The fluid should be $^3/_4$ inches into the dipstick (if provided) or to the bottom of the fill port.

- Some systems use Type A Automatic Transmission Fluid (Dexron, ATF) to refill the reservoir; other systems use hydraulic fluid. Check your documentation. Do not mix the fluids.

- Some systems need to have the fluid changed every 24 months. Check your documentation.

- The location of the reservoir varies with the model of the motorhome. Often in gas-driven models, the reservoir is in the front near the oil reservoir.

- Inspect and clean all hydraulic pump electrical connections every 12 months.

- Remove dirt and road debris from jacks as needed.

▶ If jacks are down for extended periods, spray the exposed leveling jack chrome rods with a silicone lubricant every month for protection against the elements. If in a salt air environment, use the silicone lubricant much more often.

▶ Do not use a greasy lubricant (such as Lithium) to maintain the seal on the bottom of the jack cylinder. This type of lubricant attracts and holds gravel and dirt. Use a light-weight lubricant spray.

# Chassis

## Wheel Bearings

With annual lubrication and proper care, a wheel bearing can last for many years. Best practice is to have the bearings checked with each service, lubed when necessary.

If purchasing a used motorhome, checking the wheel bearings are at the top of the list. You may need to have the bearings repacked.

## Axels, Brakes, Differential

All axels should be checked once a year. Brakes should be checked with each tire inspection, if possible. Pay particular attention when traveling near salt air, as brakes suck in the caustic air. This probably applies driving on snow-plowed roads too.

Do not forget to service the differential (if applicable) every few years.

## Engine Transmission

The transmission should be flushed every 30,000 miles, but the fluids checked every time the oil is changed.

## Engine Belts and Hoses

After purchasing a used motorhome, have all the belts and hoses checked immediately, along with an oil change and lube.

Checking the belts and hoses should also be on the pre-purchase checklist.

After retrieving from storage, always check the belts and hoses, just in case some critter has made their home inside the compartment.

## RV Slideouts

If your RV has slideouts, there are several functions to be aware of when retracting and extending them.

- Always follow the manufacturer's instructions regarding the leveling of the coach.
- If the coach is equipped with a luggage compartment beneath the room that extends, make sure the compartment doors are closed so not to interfere with the slide out operation.
- Check for obstacles or people both inside and outside the vehicle.
- Make sure all pins, safety straps, and bars have been removed and no obstructions on the inside walls or floor.

▶ Set the Park Brake.

▶ To check the hydraulic fluid, fully retract all slides. Remove the breather cap from the top of the hydraulic oil reservoir. The oil level should be approximately one inch below the top of the reservoir.

▶ See the manufacturer's instructions for the proper fluid to refill the reservoir.

▶ In an emergency, Dexron Automatic Transmission Fluid can be used. Do not use brake fluid or hydraulic jack fluid.

▶ Treat outer seals occasionally with *303 Protectant* for a smooth quiet operation.

▶ To avoid vinyl flooring scratches or carpet pile snags, clean the floors inside before retracting.

# Notes:

---

# Hot Weather Tips

## Refrigerator

When it is extremely hot outside, try parking your RV with the refrigerator side in the shade. Periodically inspect and clean the refrigerator door gaskets.

To check them for a good seal:

- Place a dollar bill behind the seal and close the door. It should stay there and not drop.
- When you try to pull it out there should be some resistance. Do this in several different places and have any damaged seals replaced.

### Install Exterior Flue Fans

If your travel plans include an extended stay in a very hot climate (over 90 degrees F daily), the refrigerator may not stay cool enough to keep food fresh.

Installing a couple of 12 V computer case fans at the top of the refrigerator vent helps eliminate this problem.

Depending on the size of your RV, there may only be room for one large fan.

Some refrigerator designs may require the fan to be installed at the bottom. Avoid this if possible. Some installers may spin a tale about the best installation, but I have tried both top and bottom vent installs and find the fans installed in the top of the vent by far outperforms the bottom location.

The top vent design is a tougher install project and may cost a few more dollars in labor, but well worth it when the temperature hits 110 degrees.

 Purchase these small computer case fans yourself at a local electronics/computer store or online (about $5 each). Do it yourself or contact a local RV repairperson to install the fans at your RV park site. Install an on/off switch for flexibility in colder climates.

**Caution**: Do not allow the installer to purchase the fans. They do not usually have the correct specifications or understand the reasoning behind using computer case fans over conventional refrigerator vent fans. Computer fans are also much less expensive ($5 versus $35).

**Note**: Unless your RV is less than 20 feet long, ignore the solar-type vent fans, as they do not produce enough airflow to do the job.

Minimum specifications to ensure high airflow and low fan noise:

**120 mm Computer Case Fan** (5 inch):
Air Flow (FM) 44.03; Max. Noise dBA) 23.5

**80 mm Computer Case Fan** (3 inch):
Air Flow (CFM) 28.89; Max Noise (dBA) 20.9

## Interior Wood Cabinets

During hot weather, leave the cabinet doors ajar to ensure ventilation and reduce warping with the temperature change as it cools off at night.

## Window Shields

To maintain cooler temperatures inside the motorhome, purchase sun shades for the windshield and other windows.

Although exterior sunshades are somewhat efficient, they are expensive, difficult and time-consuming to attach and store. You must climb a ladder to put them on and the install requires strength to stretch them across the windshield.

Spring-loaded shades work best for my windshield/cockpit windows as they snap closed and store anywhere. Silver Mylar fabric is best but nylon may be all that is available.

Blackout curtains are available at most large truck stops. These curtains have hooks that fit over the top of the main salon or bedroom window valances, just the perfect length for a motorhome.

# Notes:

# Storing Your RV

## Draining the Tanks

- ▷ Remove the drain plug on the water heater. Allow the water to drain out. Replace the plug.
- ▷ Find the drain plug on the water tank. Drain all but a few gallons. Replace the plug.
- ▷ Use potable Antifreeze in the fresh water tank to prevent freezing.

## Water Pump

- ▷ Run the water pump until it sucks air.
- ▷ Using potable Anti-freeze in the fresh water tank should prevent any problems in the lines.

## Avoiding Broken Pipes

- ▷ Keep water in the pipes P-trap.
- ▷ Each month while in storage, add a little water to the kitchen and bathroom pipes.

## Gray and Black Water Tanks

Keep a small amount of water in each tank. Pump a small amount of potable antifreeze into each tank.

## Generator

Run the generator for an hour each month. Every 50 hours, check the spark plugs. Change the oil and filter.

## Tires

- ▶ Michelin recommends that cardboard, plastic, or plywood be placed between the tire and the storage surface
- ▶ Inflate the tires to the recommended psi on the tire
- ▶ Thoroughly clean tires with soap and water
- ▶ Store out of a high ozone area
- ▶ Cover the tires, if stored in direct sunlight
- ▶ Lower the hydraulic levelers to take some of the weight off the tires

## Refrigerator

- ▶ Leave an open container of baking soda inside to absorb odors
- ▶ Prop the door open a few inches

# Windows

- Close all blinds and curtains
- Use reflective coverings inside the windows, if available

# Vents

- Leave one vent cracked for air circulation. Depending on the storage environment, all other openings should be closed
- Cover the furnace vent and hot water vents with protective screens to keep out the critters
- Close any other openings inside with rags or foam that might allow critters to enter

# Miscellaneous Items

The temperature inside a stored RV can fluctuate wildly. Expect any item stored to be affected.

- Remove any plastic items that might melt in extreme heat
- Remove any canned items, canned or bottled soda (any carbonized bottles or cans)
- Remove any cleaning items that are under pressure, such as foam cleaners, etc.
- Remove any lotions, pressurized hair sprays, etc.
- If a damp climate, provide moisture absorbing pellets or other devices

# **N**otes:

# Driving Tips

## Proper Braking Technique

The use of brakes on a long and/or steep downgrade is only a supplement to the braking effect of the engine. Here is a tip courtesy of *Escapee Magazine*.

1. When your speed increases to or above your safe speed, apply the brakes aggressively enough to feel a definite slowdown.

2. When your speed is reduced to approximately five (5) mph below your safe speed, release the brake. It should take about 7 seconds on the brake pedal to accomplish this.

3. When your speed increases again to your safe speed, repeat steps 1 and 2.

If your motorhome is gas powered, this information should help ease the tension on grades. It is usually a long, slow, haul up and a slightly scary ride down.

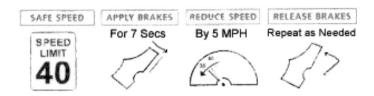

## Understanding the Gears

If in a gas-powered motorhome, watch the speed to determine when to shift on grades.

Most Chevrolet and Ford engines have four forward gears:

*Automatic Overdrive* – Normal driving without grades. When passing another vehicle at less than 35 mph, push the accelerator pedal half-way to the floor. If passing at more than 35 mph, push the pedal all the way to the floor.

*D for 3ʳᵈ Gear* – Normal driving with some steep hills. This gear can be used instead of Overdrive, but the gas consumption is greater.

*2ⁿᵈ Gear* – Used for steep grades or slow speeds for control. Do not exceed 40 mph in this gear.

*1ˢᵗ Gear* – Used for very slow speeds for control or torque. Do not exceed 30 mph.

The rule for choosing gears on grades is to use the same gear going down as when climbing. Use your best judgment on this.

*It is important to select the proper gear before starting the down-grade.* You may find it impossible to down shift at high speeds.

If following the proper braking technique as discussed above, you and the engine arrive safely at the bottom of the grade, no fear.

According to some sources, the 2500 to 3500 RPM range is the happy place for most gas-powered engines. This means that if the RPMs drop into the lower range, the engine is getting more wear than necessary.

However, when towing, my Chevrolet 454 is happy at 2000 RPM (55 mph legal towing speed in California and many other states). Find the happy place for your engine and stick with it no matter what the pundits say.

## Speed Limits

Speed limits vary from state to state when towing something behind the motorhome. Always stick to the legal limit as some counties can be aggressive with traffic violations.

The speed limit posted at a freeway offramp indicates the speed you should be driving when you make the turn. It is very difficult to go from 55 to 30 in a few seconds, but be aware that is expected. These posted limits are obviously not designed for RVs or 16-wheelers.

# Adjusting Outside Mirrors

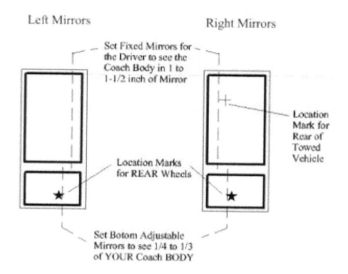

Courtesy of Don Bobbitt

Adjusting the large side mirrors on your motorhome are similar to your automobile. The difference is that the motorhome has broken the scene in the mirror down into two pieces.

The top mirror looks down the side of the motorhome (just like in your car), but the bottom mirror looks down to the road and back, so you can see your rear wheels.

The bottom mirror also allows you to see any auto coming up alongside into what would be your blind spot.

## Backing with the Stars

In the illustration, note the stars in the bottom mirrors. These stars are very helpful markers when backing into a site.

Have someone stand at the rear wheel well. Place the star on the bottom mirror where their knees are reflected. Repeat this on the other side or use the awning arm (if over the wheel well).

# Pivot Point When Turning

The pivot point is in the center of the rear axle. This is an important point to recognize so you can see how the motorhome rotates around a turn. If any stationary object, like a tree, is at the center of the rear axle, you do not hit it when you turn.

## Tail Swing

The "tail swing" is the distance behind the pivot point that the body of the motorhome moves in the opposite direction of the front when turning.

To measure the swing distance, stop the motorhome along a straight line. Make a complete turn away from the line. Have someone else measure the maximum swing as you turn.

An excellent time to do this is during your RV driving class. Have the instructor measure the swing for you. Part of a driving class curriculum is to help you judge when to setup to start a backing turn.

## Cargo Weight Balance

One of the major causes of accidents with recreational vehicles of any kind is the imbalance of weight. It is very important to get the RV weighed at the first opportunity.

Some commercial scales allow RVs to weigh the front and back separately. There is sometimes a charge, but often it is a public service.

Before you can get the feel of how much stopping time is necessary, you must understand the weight balance. When making even the smallest turn, the weight balance comes into play.

You already have experienced items that become projectiles when thrown around. These are now stowed. The next step is getting the feel of the weight distribution in the cabinets and outside compartments.

When the levelers are extended, if you always extend one side more than the other, this is a sign of weight imbalance.

> ▶ Get the RV weighed as soon as possible. Pull into the nearest commercial highway scales station; visit a major RV rally and look for a vendor; call around to truck repair shops (or check the yellow pages) to find the nearest scale.
> ▶ Fix any imbalance by shifting something as innocent as canned goods, sporting goods, heavy dinnerware...you get the picture.

RV manufacturers are supposed to put weight balance at the top of the list when they design the interior. The chassis is rated for the maximum load.

This is expressed in the following cryptic symbols, courtesy of the *RV Safety & Education Foundation*:

## GVWR

**Gross Vehicle Weight Rating** is the **maximum** allowable weight of the fully loading vehicle, including liquids, passengers, cargo, and the tongue weight of any towed vehicle.

## GAWR

**Gross Axel Weight Rating** is the **maximum** allowable weight each axle assembly is designed to carry, measured at the tires. This includes the weight of the axle assembly (tires, wheels, springs, axle).

This rating assumes that the load is equal on each side. It is also established by rating the axle assembly on the weakest link.

## GCWR

**Gross Combination Weight Rating** is the **maximum allowable combined weight** of the tow vehicle and the attached towed vehicle. This rating assumes that both vehicles have functioning brakes.

## GTWR

**Gross Trailer Weight Rating** is the **maximum** towed vehicle weight. Each component (receiver, drawbar, ball) of a ball-type hitch has its own rating.

Some ball-type hitches have separate ratings when used with a weight distributing system.

## TWR/TLR/LR

**Tongue Weight, Tongue Load,** and **Vertical Load Rating** are different terms for the **maximum vertical load** that can be carried by the hitch.

## Tire Ratings

The **maximum** load that a tire may carry is engraved on the sidewall, along with a corresponding cold inflation pressure. A reduction in inflation pressure requires a reduction in load rating. In other words, keep the RV tires as the highest maximum psi allowed.

## UVW

**Unloaded Vehicle** is the weight of a vehicle as built at the factory with full fuel, engine/generator oil and coolants. It **does not include** cargo, fresh water, LP gas, occupants, or dealer installed accessories.

## NCC

**Net Carrying** is the **maximum** weight of all personal belongings, food, fresh water, LP gas, tools, and dealer installed accessories that can be carried by the RV.

## SCWR

**Sleeping Capacity Weight Rating** is the manufacturers designated **number of sleeping positions** multiplied by 154 pounds (70 kilograms).

## CCC

**Cargo Carrying Capacity** is equal to **GVWR minus** each of the following: **UVW**, full fresh potable water weight (including the water in the water heater), full LP gas weight, and **SCWR**.

# Liquid Weights (Pounds per Gallon)

- Water: 8.3
- Gasoline: 5.6
- Diesel Fuel: 6.8
- Propane: 4.2 at 60 degrees F (expanding at 1.5 percent per ten degrees Fahrenheit)

Follow Margo's blog, *http://MovingOnWithMargo.com*

# eBooks by Margo Armstrong
Available at these fine eBookstores: Amazon, Barnes&Noble, Kobo, Apple

**RV LIFESTYLE COLLECTION**
* Conquer the Road – RV Maintenance for Travelers
* *How To Save Money While Enjoying The RV Lifestyle*
* *For Women Only - Traveling Solo In Your RV, The Adventure of a Lifetime*
* *For Women Only – Motorhome Care & Maintenance*
* *Selling Online - Supporting the Traveling Lifestyle*
* *Staying In Touch, A Traveler's Guide*
* *The RV Lifestyle - A Dream Come True*
* *Working On The Road - For Professionals and Just Fun-Loving Folks*

**TRAVEL**
* *Welcome to Las Vegas - The Essential Guide*

**WRITING EBOOKS**
* *Writing & Publishing eBooks - One Person's Journey*

**TOOLS FOR LIVING COLLECTION**
* *Get Amazing Photos From Your Point & Shoot Camera*
* *Buying and Selling Gold and Silver - A Primer for the Beginning Investor*
* *Selling Your Home - How the Real Estate Market Works*
* *Do Your Own Probate - Summary Administration for Small Estates*

**WOMEN'S STUDIES COLLECTION**
* *Answering the Call - Women in Action, Vol 1: Leaders in the World*
* *Answering the Call - Women in Action, Vol 2: Leaders in America*
* *About Men - Myths Revealed, How to Love, Live, and Work With Them*
* *For Women Only - Traveling Solo In Your RV, The Adventure of a Lifetime*
* *For Women Only - Buying and Selling Gold & Silver*
* *For Women Only – Motorhome Care & Maintenance*

**FOOD FOR THOUGHT**
* *What Determines Our Destiny*

CPSIA information can be obtained
at www.ICGtesting.com
Printed in the USA
FSHW020531190419
57403FS